Why Don't Sheep Shrink When It Rains?

Why Don't Sheep Shrink When It Rains?

A Further Collection of Photocopier Folklore

Alan Dundes & Carl R. Pagter

Syracuse University Press

Copyright © 2000 by Syracuse University Press
Syracuse, New York 13244-5160

All Rights Reserved

First Edition 2000

00 01 02 03 04 05   6 5 4 3 2 1

The paper used in this publication meets the minimum requirements of American National Standard for Information Sciences—Permanence of Paper for Printed Library Materials, ANSI Z39.48-1984.

Library of Congress Cataloging-in-Publication Data

Dundes, Alan.
    Why don't sheep shrink when it rains? : a further collection of photocopier folklore / Alan Dundes & Carl R. Pagter. — 1st ed.
      p.   cm.
    ISBN 0-8156-0600-1 (paper : alk. paper)
    1. Folklore—United States. 2. Urban folklore—United States. 3. American wit and humor. 4. Office practice—United States—Folklore. I. Pagter, Carl R., 1934– . II. Title.
GR105.D88 1999
398.2'0973'091732—dc21   99-32839

Manufactured in the United States of America

Contents

Preface   xiii
Editor's Note   xv
Introduction   xvii
Abbreviations   xix

Off the Wall

1. Thank You for Not Smoking   2
2. Thank You for Holding   5
3. Swine Flu Notice   6
4. To Whom It May Concern   7
5. One Person Per Day   8
6. This Is *Not* Burger King   10
7. Smile and Be Happy   13
8. We've Upped Our Standards   14
9. Prices Subject to Change   15
10. The Customer Is Always Right   16
11. Everyone Brings Joy to This Room   17
12. Have a Nice Day   18
13. Your Mother Does Not Work Here   19
14. We Trained Hard   20
15. Tomorrow We've Got to Get Organized   21
16. Are You Lonely?   22
17. There Is No Pleasure   24
18. I Did It Right the First Time   25
19. The Last Revision   29
20. Make One More Change!   31

21. Go Ahead   35
22. The Hawaiian Gourmet & Luau Society   37
23. The Airport Commission Is Pleased to Announce   38
24. To Get Along in This World   39
25. How to Get Along at the Office   40
26. Lord, Grant Me the Serenity   41
27. Take Care!!!   43
28. There Is No Evidence   45
29. Quality Is Like Buying Oats   46
30. Can You Make This Thing Work?   48
31. No Machine Can Do My Job   49
32. Notice to All Employees   51
33. Happiness Is . . .   52
34. Doing a Good Job Here   53
35. This Job Is a Test   60
36. Enjoy Life   61
37. If You Have to Walk on Thin Ice   62
38. Thank You and Goodbye   63
39. Remember Me?   64

Wordplay

40. Clinton Deploys Vowels to Bosnia   66
41. Who Makxs a Group a Succxss?   68
42. You Foul-Mouthed Swine   69
43. Welcome to the Psychiatric Hot Line   70
44. Word Association   72
45. Straight Man Test   73
46. T-Shirts in Castro Street Shops   75
47. Country Songs   76
48. I Love Country Music   78
49. Reasons Why E-Mail Is Like a Penis   79
50. 3 Kinds of Sex   80
51. Four Things That Resemble . . .   81
52. Five Reasons Why It's a Bummer To Be an Egg   82
53. A Short Course in Human Relations   84
54. Seven Reasons Why Chicago Is Quiet on Sundays   85

55. The Last 10 Things   86
56. How Dogs and Men Are the Same   89
57. What Are the Ten Biggest Lies?   95
58. 101 Things Not to Say During Sex   96
59. Handling Skepticism in Large Crowds   99
60. His Driveway Doesn't Go All the Way Out to the Street   100
61. Euphemisms for "Self Gratification"   104
62. The Elementary School   105
63. Dyslexics Repent!   107
64. Learning to Spell with "Darnell"   109
65. Hebonics   115
66. Rune-Sore-Bees?   117
67. The Little Rascals   119
68. Questions of Life   120
69. Proof That Horses Have an Infinite Number of Legs   126
70. The Bumblebee Cannot Fly   127
71. The Chicken Gun   129
72. ValueJet Advertising Slogans   130
73. Dear Captayn   134
74. What the Captain Means Is...   135
75. I Am Their Leader!   141
76. Welcome to...   142
77. Yugo's, Ford Escorts,...   144
78. Van Gogh's Family   145
79. Actual Advertisements   147
80. The Passing of the Energizer Bunny   149
81. What Is This?   151

From the Funny File

82. Please Divert Your Course   154
83. Mad Dogs and Englishmen   156
84. Honk If You Love Jesus   158
85. Schnauzer   160
86. You Read It Here First   161
87. We Could Have Saved the Bentley   163
88. Another Wife Story   165

89. Game Time   166
90. Chinese Torture Test   167
91. How'd You Break Your Arm?   168
92. Blondes   170
93. Dumb Men Jokes   177
94. You Are Now a Woman   180
95. MENtal Anxiety   181
96. He's Shaving You Right Now   182
97. Guess What?   183
98. Do I Know 'Array' Awkins?   185
99. A Nun Gets on a Bus   186
100. Three Dogs   188
101. Martians   189
102. If the Truth Be Known   190
103. How to Make $75,000 a Day   192
104. I Cut, I Cut   194
105. The Old Miser   196
106. I Will Grant You Three Wishes   197
107. Kingsview Mental Hospital   199
108. Parrot Boss   200
109. A Short Day   201
110. Jesus Is Watching You   202
111. A Commuter on The London Underground   203
112. Lion Tamer Audition   204

Offbeat Beasthood

113. Pick the Winning Racehorse!   208
114. Whoa!   210
115. Attitude   212
116. It's Been a Great Year   213
117. How to Housebreak Your Dog   214
118. Lonely at the Top   218
119. Louisiana Mosquito   219
120. How Easter Eggs Are Made!!!   220
121. As Much as I Can Stand   222
122. Gathering Nuts   223

123. Mouse Balls 225
124. Computer Mouse 226
125. She Was a Tough One 228
126. What Are You Laughing At? 230
127. What Happens from Drinking Too Much Milk 236
128. A "Cow" Boy 240
129. Stuffing the Turkey 242
130. The Italian Lover 244
131. Stop Crying Mary 247
132. The Line-Up 248
133. The Shepherd 249
134. Italian Duck Call 251
135. Miss America Duck Call 254
136. Fetch the Duck 256
137. Dear Diary 257
138. The Deer Hunt 262
139. Basic Rules for Deer Hunting 264
140. I Think I Just Heard a Buck Snort! 265
141. Here's Your Deer Meat 266
142. This One's Barely Legal!! 268
143. Fisherman's Prayer 272

Pictorial Picks

144. There Must Be More to Life 274
145. Jammed Again 275
146. The Computer Broke Down 276
147. Who's Got the Brain Today? 277
148. Burned Out 278
149. Tired of Your Job??? 279
150. Greetings from California 283
151. Please, Do Go on with Your Story 284
152. Let Go Me Ankles, Murphy 286
153. Thermometers in the Refrigerator 287
154. In Order to Speed Your Recovery 288
155. Your Bedpan, Sir!! 289
156. Hillary Clinton Health Care Reform 293

157. Mothers!! 295
158. The Birth of a Salesman 296
159. No! I Can't Be Bothered 297
160. Air Bag 299
161. Are You Sure That's a Breathalizer? 301
162. Next Time, Use All of Your Fingers 305
163. Are You Stuck? 306
164. Can I Have a Grant? 307
165. Deadline? 308
166. Help Wanted Male 309
167. Application for Pardon 311
168. Pervert of the Year Award 312
169. The *Perfect* Man 313
170. Waiting . . . for the Perfect Man 314
171. Perfection 315
172. The Little Woman 316
173. The Perfect Day 318
174. Stop Exaggerating 319
175. Before It Gets Soft! 321
176. No—I Can't Go Bowling Tonight 323
177. Golf Balls 324
178. Here, Take These 325
179. Footprints 327
180. The Beginning and the End 329

Conclusions 331

Alan Dundes and Carl R. Pagter are the authors of *Work Hard and You Shall Be Rewarded, When You're Up to Your Ass in Alligators, Never Try to Teach a Pig to Sing,* and *Sometimes the Dragon Wins.* Dundes is a professor of anthropology and folklore at the University of California, Berkeley, and Pagter is a retired attorney.

Preface

We would like to gratefully recognize and thank all of the many individuals who have supplied us with the materials found in this volume. Without their continuing assistance, we would not have compiled this, our fifth, sampling of the rich tradition of photocopier folklore. Although the majority of the items received by us turn out to be duplicates (often with variation), we are nevertheless always pleased to see them as they confirm the traditionality of the items and demonstrate their ongoing currency. The fact that our contributors are spread throughout the United States at once provides us with evidence of regional difference as well as the breadth of the geographical distribution of particular items. Although we do not refer to individual contributors item by item, we do list geographical provenience and date of each item whenever possible.

We wish to express our gratitude to each of the following: Esther Anderson, Gerry Andre, Josephine Biley Andrion, Bob Armstrong, Karen Baker, Carl Banker, Devora Belilove, Michael E. Bell, Phyllis Bischof, Andrew Burdon, Chick Berkstresser, Barbara Bills, Carol Bird, Sue Bonderant, Patti Breitman, Alexandria Buckner, Joyce Bungert, Paula Burns, Gay Callan, Malcolm Campbell, Simon J. Carmel, Sharon Chan, Johnny Chang, James Chung, Sheila R. Chung, Doug Coe, Roy Colegrove, Alicia Contic, Barry Cooper, Lee Davis, Michael Davison, Stacy Dobrzensky, James F. Drahos, Lauren Dundes, Catherine Elliott, Marcella Espenschide, Rocio Ferreira, Marsha Franklin, Derek Froome, Lisa Gentry, Dorothy Gillim, Shirley Gillim, David Goines, Francis Hall, David Hanzel, Clare Hartley, George Hempstead, Kalista Hickman, Bob Hoenisch, Judy Holt, David Hunn, J. Summer Kalwani, Juris Kanasevics, Joey Keathley, Wally Killian, Kathy Kirkpatrick, Uli Kutter, D. Lee Kvalnes, Marisa La Dou, Brian Lee, Ryan Liebenberg, Cindy Littell, Leonard B. Loeb, Peter Louett, Rebecca Maksel, Larry Marks, Alfra Martini, Virginia Matzek, Esther May, Lorne Mellors, Ron Mesing, William E. Metzel,

Nancy Michael, Wolfgang Mieder, Esther L. Miguel, Margo Miller, Katie Milton, John Mott, Bob Murphy, Carrie Musolff, Tom O'Connor, Mark Ohno, Thomas K. O'Karma, Tammy Page, Ed and Joanne Pagter, Judie Pagter, Ralph G. Pagter, S. J. ("Joe") Park, Amanda Peterson, Robin Polk, Susie Prausnitz, Paul Renteln, Cynthia Rickards, William Rodarmor, Edith T. Rowe, Mary Runge, Jenny Schulz, Jason Shiga, Curtis Shirley, David Sidd, Richard Sims, Steve Siporin, Kira Blaisdell-Sloan, Moira Smith, Asa Sparks, Tiffany Spencer, Eileen Starr, Frank Strnad, John Talbot, Peter Tamony, Jim Theodores, B. F. ("Tommy") Thompson, Jr., Joseph F. Tuso, Barbara Vestal, Howard Weber, Susan Weiss, Paige Wentworth, Sue Williams, Barry R. Willis, Ann Wonder, and Tyrone Wong.

Special recognition and our heartfelt thanks to Bob Hoenisch, D. Lee Kvalnes, Asa Sparks, Frank Strnad and Tyrone Wong, each of whom contributed four or more items used in this collection, and especially to Esther Anderson, Carl Banker, Joyce Bungert, David Goines, George Hempstead, Nancy Michael, John Mott, and Bob Murphy, who each contributed nine or more items. Without the extraordinary support of these friends, this collection could not have been realized.

Editor's Note

We have followed the format utilized in our previous four volumes. With few exceptions, the items bear no indication of attribution. Obviously every item was created at some point in time, but through the process known as "communal re-creation" the item gradually evolves such that it may differ markedly from its original form. In any case, the original author or cartoonist's name disappears in the process. It should also be noted that while the folk may borrow freely from whatever sources they choose (including published or authored works), it is also true that creative writers borrow just as freely from folklore materials in the public domain. The latter practice may account in part for the competing claims of authorship for an item. Virtually all of our data are of anonymous authorship and one of the reasons why we choose to include multiple versions of items is to demonstrate conclusively that there is no one single creator of these items. Since relatively few items out of all those that are composed are accepted, so to speak, by the folk for inclusion in their collective repertoire, such acceptance can be construed as a high honor as it constitutes a kind of validation or judgment of an item's intrinsic value and appeal.

We have intentionally not corrected obvious misspellings or grammatical errors inasmuch as doing so would reduce the authenticity and value of the data we present. We have also made it a point not to exclude items which might be construed by some as offensive or tasteless. Photocopier folklore, like all folklore, is relatively immune from censorship. This inevitably presents a problem when folklorists seek to publish such materials. The censorship of published materials is a long-standing obstacle in folklore scholarship. Nineteenth and for that matter twentieth century folklorists either expurgated their folkloristic texts or simply omitted them from their published collections. We feel that it is intellectually dishonest and we make no apology for the materials included in this volume. It is our goal to document a vital form of American folklore.

In that context, we owe a special debt to Syracuse University Press for publishing this and our previous collection *Sometimes the Dragon Wins* (1996). In particular, we cannot adequately express our sincere appreciation to Dr. Robert A. Mandel, the director of Syracuse University Press, for his encouragement and courage in facilitating the recording and preservation of these remarkable forms of modern Americana.

Introduction

For the past thirty odd years, we have been keenly interested in observing the technological influence on the transmission of certain types of written folklore. During the nineteenth century, such items were passed on by means of laboriously handwritten copies. Print shops would occasionally issue sub rosa broad-sheets or cards containing traditional material intended for private distribution. Later developments such as the typewriter and the mimeograph machine, derived in part from an invention of none other than Thomas A. Edison, made it possible for individuals to reproduce such items more easily. Technology continued to evolve in the twentieth century with the appearance of the photocopier. By the end of the twentieth century, the availability of the facsimile machine known as the FAX, Electronic or E Mail, and Personal Computers greatly facilitated the rapid if not instant transmission of written items. The advent of the Internet, which connects myriads of individual Personal Computers, further accelerated the exchange of information, including many items of folklore. As a result of this technological evolution or should we say revolution, there has been a burgeoning transmission of the items contained in this volume. Individuals armed with this technology no longer have to depend upon small print shops to circulate favorite items to their circles of friends. Access to the Internet has greatly simplified the whole processes of obtaining copies of such items. There are many more examples of E-Mail and Internet versions of folklore in this volume than in any of our previous collections.

In some instances, we include several versions of an item to illustrate the fascinating degree of variation as well as geographical distribution. Where possible, we note parallels appearing in print in both scholarly and popular sources. Unfortunately, most of the popular anthologies of this sort of material make no attempt to do anything more than present unadorned texts. There is no critical commentary whatsoever. Each of the items contained in this volume deserves in-depth study. In a sampling of the photocopier tradition consisting of nearly two hundred distinct items, it is not possible to offer a full-scale analysis of so many texts. However, it is our belief that as more and more professional folklorists come to appreciate these remarkable instances of modern folklore, they will become the subjects of intensive scholarly investigations. Just as there are monographs devoted to individual ballads or folktales, there will be analytic essays probing individual photocopier-folklore items.

For ease of presentation, we have somewhat arbitrarily divided our corpus into five general sections. The first titled "Off the Wall," basically features material one might find on an office wall, bulletin board, or desk blotter. The second section, "Word Play," contains various traditional verbal creations full of wit and humor. The third grouping, "From the Funny File," includes those jokes that are circulated by the office copier or other mechanical means. The penultimate section, "Offbeat Beasthood," focuses on items involving animals. The last chapter, "Pictorial Picks," contains folk cartoons, one of the most popular genres of photocopier folklore.

We see absolutely no indication of any diminution of the creation and flow of photocopier folklore. Quite the contrary, as we have indicated, the succession of technological innovations in data transmission have encouraged more, not less, photocopier folklore. Moreover, as international communication continues to expand, it is very likely that some of the items will attain near worldwide circulation. To be sure, there are still areas of the world where modern technology remains a rarity, but as technology spreads, so also does the folklore spawned by it. Accordingly, the reporting and eventually the serious study of photocopier folklore may well become a worldwide venture.

Abbreviations

Wherever possible, we have tried to locate parallel cognate versions of the items included in this volume. Because there are still relatively few major collections of folklore transmitted by office copier machines, we have elected to list these collections here. Since we cite some of these sources throughout our volume, we have used the following abbreviations:

CS	Else Marie Kofod, *Chefens Sekretaer Og andre beske kommentarer til hverdagens fortaedeligheder* (Aalborg: Det Schonbergske Forlag, 1988)
FOJ1	Adam Warlock, *250 Funniest Office Jokes, Memos & Cartoon Pinups* (Collinsville, Illinois: Knightraven Books, 1993)
FOJ2	Adam Warlock, *250 Funniest Office Jokes, Memors & Cartoon Pinups*, Volume 2 (Collinsville, Illinois: Knightbraven Books, 1995)
IK	Uli Kutter, *Ich Kundige!!! Zeugnisse von Wünscheri und Ängsten am Arbeitsplatz—Eine Bestandsaufnahme* (Marburg: Jonas Verlag, 1982)
ISR	Institute for Sex Research, 416 Morrison Hall, Indiana University, Bloomington, Indiana 47401
MF	Ulf Palmenfelt, *Modern Folkhumor: Folkhumor I fotostat* (Stockholm: Bokfölaget, Prisma, 1986)
NLM	G. Legman, *No Laughing Matter: Rationale of the Dirty Joke An Analysis of Sexual Humor,* Second Series (New York: Breaking Point, 1975)
NT	Alan Dundes and Carl R. Pagter, *Never Try to Teach A Pig To Sing: Still More Urban Folklore from the Paperwork Empire* (Detroit: Wayne State University Press, 1991)

OG2	Nicolas Locke, *Office Graffiti 2* (London: Proteus Books, 1981)
OHB	Pete Fagan and Mark Schaffer, *The Office Humour Book* (London: Angus and Robertson, 1986)
OH2	Pete Fagan and Mark Schaffer, *Office Humor II* (New York: Harmony Books, 1992)
RDJ	G. Legman, *Rationale of the Dirty Joke—An Analysis of Sexual Humor,* First Series (New York: Grove Press, 1968)
RIF	Paul Smith, *Reproduction Is Fun* (London: Routledge and Kegan Paul, 1986)
RJ	*Rugby Jokes in the Office* (London: Sphere Books, 1989)
SD	Alan Dundes and Carl R. Pagter, *Sometimes the Dragon Wins: Yet More Urban Folklore From the Paperwork Empire* (Syracuse: Syracuse University Press, 1996)
SS	Ulla Lipponen, *Siistiä Sisätyötä: Kopiohuumoria* (Helsinki: Suomalaisen Kirjallisuuden Seura, 1989)
TCB	Paul Smith, *The Complete Book of Office MisPractice* (London: Routledge and Kegan Paul, 1984)
UFFC-PC	Louis Michael Bell, Cathy Makin Orr, and Michael James Preston, *Urban Folklore from Colorado: Photocopy Cartoons* (Ann Arbor: Xerox University Microfilms, 1976)
UFFC-TB	Cathy Makin Orr and Michael James Preston, *Urban Folklore from Colorado: Typescript Broadsides* (Ann Arbor: Xerox University Microfilms, 1976)
UOH	S. E. Mills, *Underground Office Humor* (New York: Citadel Press, 1994)
WH	Alan Dundes and Carl R. Pagter, *Work Hard and You Shall Be Rewarded: Urban Folklore from the Paperwork Empire* (Bloomington: Indiana University Press, 1978)
WY	Alan Dundes and Carl R. Pagter, *When You're Up to Your Ass in Alligators... More Urban Folklore from the Paperwork Empire* (Detroit: Wayne State University Press, 1987)
YD	Wayne B. Norris, *You Don't Have to Be Crazy to Work Here... But It Sure Helps* (Los Angeles: Price/Stern/Sloan, 1986)
YWIW	Nicolas Locke, *You Want It When?!! The Complete Office Graffiti* (London: Proteus Books, 1979)

Why Don't Sheep Shrink When It Rains?

Off the Wall

In and among official notices posted on bulletin boards one not infrequently finds folklore items. They range from notice parodies to purported slogans to pseudo proverbial advice. Some office managers frown on these materials and demand that employees refrain from cluttering their walls with such unofficial decoration. In other offices, employees may express themselves partly through the display of folklore items in their immediate surroundings. Because most of these items are open to public view, they are not as sexually or ethnically charged as some other photocopier folklore. Rather they tend to be mainly anti-establishment, anti-bureaucracy in theme.

1. Thank You for Not Smoking

One of the principal public health issues of the late twentieth century concerned the carcinogenic effect of cigarettes not only on the smoker but on those persons in the vicinity of the smoker. The discovery that secondhand smoke could be deleterious to a non-smoker's health has led to the banning of smoking in public places in many states. Even where smoking is not formally interdicted by law, it has become common courtesy for would-be smokers to first ask for permission from those around them. In many offices where smoking is still legally permitted, the non-smoking occupants may request that their colleagues refrain from doing so, perhaps with a direct polite sign thanking them in advance for not lighting up. In folk tradition, in a time of reduced civility a simple request may not suffice. Our first text, collected in Iselin, New Jersey, in 1992, aggressively demands that the reader of the notice not smoke. A second text from Wilmington, Delaware, in 1991, represents a smoker's equally aggressive rebuttal. A third text on the same theme, collected in Virginia in 1990, constitutes a nonsmoker's final rebuttal. It also suggests that the smoker's formulaic "Mind if I smoke?" is insincere inasmuch as he is depicted with a lighted cigarette already in his mouth.

THANK YOU FOR NOT SMOKING

CIGARETTE SMOKE IS THE RESIDUE OF YOUR PLEASURE
IT POLUTES THE AIR, CONTAMINATES MY HAIR,
AND DIRTIES MY CLOTHES, NOT TO MENTION
WHAT IT DOES TO MY LUNGS
IT TAKES PLACE WITHOUT MY CONSENT

I HAVE A PLEASURE ALSO: I LIKE BEER NOW AND THEN
THE RESIDUE OF MY PLEASURE IS URINE
WOULD YOU BE ANNOYED IF I STOOD ON A CHAIR
WITHOUT YOUR CONSENT
AND PISSED ON YOUR HEAD?
THANK YOU FOR YOUR UNDERSTANDING

THANK YOU FOR HOLDING YOUR BREATH WHILE I'M SMOKING

2. Thank You for Holding

Another insincere formula all too common in modern-day bureaucracy pretends to apologize for putting a telephone caller on hold. It is one thing to wait for a minute or so to reach one's party, but it is quite another to be put on hold indefinitely—often to the accompaniment of unwelcome music or annoying commercials. Instead of offering to take the caller's number and call him or her back, the harried operator or secretary rudely wastes the caller's time by placing him or her on extended hold. The caller could in theory hang up and call again, but there is always the hope that the hold is about to come to an end plus the likelihood that another attempt to call would have the same unsatisfactory result.

This text was collected at the Central Health Center in Oakland, California in 1994. Other versions include a computer screen with a similar telephone image. For another cartoon with a waiting skeleton, see WY, 204.

3. Swine Flu Notice

Annually, there is a threat of an influenza or flu epidemic. There are different varieties of the virus that predominate within a given year. Sometimes a new strain will appear, a strain not covered by a standard flu inoculation. The following item, collected in Ontario, Canada, in 1994, is a parody of an announcement issued by the Ontario Ministry of Health warning of a possible outbreak of swine flu.

Ontario — Ministry of Health — **bulletin** — Ontario Health Insurance Plan

Bulletin number:	Date:	Direct Inquiries:
665	730054	January 5, 1985	— P. I. Gibbons
Distribution: Physicians, Hospitals, Clinics and Labs		(see also below)

DEPARTMENT OF PUBLIC HEALTH

NOTICE

Memo to: Ottawa Residents and areas within 200 miles

Subject: Swine Flu

As you know, there is a possibility of an outbreak of Swine Flu in this area.

In order that you may be on the alert for indications that you or members of your family may have contacted the virus, you should be aware of the following symptoms:

1. Sore throat
2. Slight headache
3. Moderate to high temperature
4. Nausea or upset stomach
5. An uncontrollable urge to fuck in the mud.

4. To Whom It May Concern

At any one point in time, there is almost certain to be tension between governmental regulation and the conduct of business enterprises. Some individuals favor more—rather than less—regulation in order to protect the consumer and to ensure public safety; others feel that the government is unnecessarily intrusive such that it seriously impedes profitable and efficient day-to-day business operations. One such governmental regulatory agency, OSHA, is charged with the duty to enforce safety and health measures in industry on a federal scale. The following item found on the wall of the main office of the UC Berkeley Campus Police in 1990 parodies a common type of safety regulation. The implication is that the consumer's or client's dissatisfaction is to be blamed on the federal agency rather than the local office. This popular item, alternatively titled "Bulletin" or "Notice," is reported coast-to-coast.

To Whom it May Concern:

The Occupational Safety and Health Administration (OSHA) has determined that the maximum safe load capacity (MSL Cap) on my butt is 2 persons at one time, unless I install footholds, handrails and safety straps.

As you have arrived 6th in line to ride my ass today, please take a number and wait your turn.

Thank You!

5. One Person Per Day

Even without federal regulations restricting the number of persons to be accommodated or served, office personnel may on their own offer minimal assistance. The following item, collected in Savage, Minnesota, in 1994, pretends to explain why a customer or coworker must forego any chance of receiving help. For another version, see FOJ2, 311.

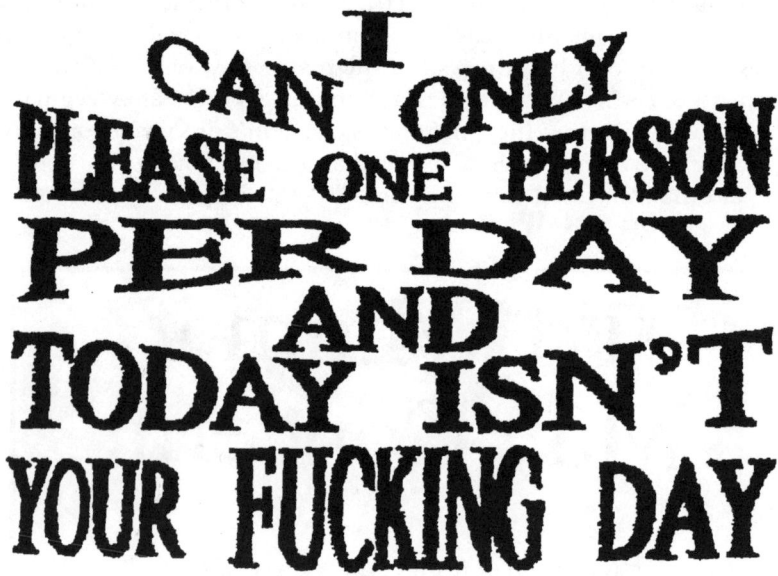

I can only please one person per day. Today is not your day. Tomorrow doesn't look good either.

6. This Is Not Burger King

Fast food franchises have proliferated exponentially. As there is more and more competition, advertising has become ever more important. One of the best known hamburger chains is Burger King, and its advertisements often emphasize the customer's right to individualize his or her order. In theory, one could ask for a hamburger medium rare with or without onions, lettuce, tomato, etc. and expect to get it exactly as ordered. In practice, customized fast food service is difficult to achieve. The employees on the front line, so to speak, may not be able to fulfill the corporate philosophy of customer choice.

The first version of the following item was collected in Chicago, in 1944; the second from North Haven, Connecticut, in 1996; while the third comes from north central Pennsylvania in 1990. There is remarkable variation in these three versions of this nationally known piece of photocopier folklore. A fourth text from Downsville, New York, in 1996, is a parody of the same chain's advertising. One of Burger King's leading sellers is a large hamburger which they dub a "Whopper." Many food chains in order to be competitive, offer various incentives, e.g., a free drink or free French Fries. Both these features are lampooned in the fourth text. For other versions, see UOM, 56.

NOTICE!

THIS IS NOT BURGER KING. YOU GET IT MY WAY OR YOU DON'T GET THE SON-OF-A-BITCH AT ALL.

**This is Not Burger King
you don't get it Your Way**

**You take it My Way or
you don't get the
Son of a Bitch!**

BURGER KINK

AREN'T YOU HORNY?

Buy a Whopper, get a blowjob free.

Please present this coupon before ordering. Limit one coupon per customer. Not to be used with other coupons or offers. Void where prohibited by law.

7. Smile and Be Happy

Whereas America is famous for being a land of optimism with Americans convinced that, as the proverb promises, "Everything will turn out for the best," citizens of other nations may hold a more realistic or cynical point of view. The following item, collected in Altrincham in Cheshire, England, in 1978, reflects more of a pessimistic worldview, the smiling face notwithstanding. For another version, see YWIW, 84.

Out of the gloom a voice said unto me "Smile and be happy: things could be worse" So I smiled and was happy and behold things did get worse!

8. We've Upped Our Standards

Part of progress includes improvement. This holds for business as well as for personal development. The following item, collected in Oakland, California, in 1990, boasts of raised standards. At the same time, it articulates an aggressive insult under the guise of inviting the addressee to raise his or her standards as well.

> # WE'VE UPPED OUR STANDARDS.
>
> # NOW UP YOURS!

9. Prices Subject to Change

In American culture, prices are usually fixed, meaning that there is little or no possibility of negotiation. This is different from many cultures in the world where one is expected to bargain in the absence of any price tag. The following item from the San Francisco Bay Area in the early 1990s pretends that prices can be affected by customer behavior.

NOTICE

Prices Subject To Change According To Customer's Attitude

10. The Customer Is Always Right

There is a well known American proverb which proclaims that "The customer is always right" (see Wolfgang Mieder et al., *A Dictionary of American Proverbs* [New York: Oxford University Press, 1992], 132). The basic premise is that a businessman cannot afford to alienate a prospective client and that therefore he should respect or at least tolerate the client's demands. On the other hand, the reality is that some buyers may make unreasonable requests or register illegitimate complaints. The following item from Menlo Park in 1991 undercuts the proverb in question, revealing what the businessman really thinks of his customer.

11. Everyone Brings Joy to This Room

A relatively polite way of telling a visitor that he may not be welcome is effectively communicated by the following item found in the University of California, Berkeley, Extension Building in 1978. Presumably each visitor has to decide the category into which he appropriately fits. For another version, see OH2, [71].

> **EVERYONE Brings Joy To This Room**
>
> *SOME BY ENTERING*
>
> *SOME BY LEAVING!*

12. Have a Nice Day

One of the most trite formulas in American folk phraseology is "Have A Nice Day" normally uttered when one person takes his leave of another. It is literally a well-meaning wish, but its use is so perfunctory as to render it platitudinous. The following two wallet cards collected in the San Francisco Bay Area in the early 1980s undercut the cliché. For other photocopier items referring to the same idiom, see SD, 27–28.

13. Your Mother Does Not Work Here

An important part of growing up should entail learning to take care of oneself including a minimum degree of cleanliness and neatness. Some individuals, however, never do seem to grow up in this respect. The following text, collected in Mountain View, California, in 1990, is meant to be a reminder to such individuals. For another version, see RIF, 143.

14. We Trained Hard

One characteristic of many bureaucracies is a foolish tendency to change for the sake of change, that is, to institute change without achieving any substantive improvement. Each change of political administration, military commanding officer, or boss in any office may produce an endless series of reshuffling and reorganizational measures. Some of them are undoubtedly necessary, but a great many of them are not. Too often, motion is confused with progress.

A notice that comments upon such needless change is attributed to Petronius Arbiter, perhaps best known for his celebrated *Satyricon*. Since Petronius supposedly died in A.D. 66, a date which does appear on some versions of this item, the date in the following version of 210 B.C. is obviously false, as is, almost certainly, the entire attribution. Versions have been collected from both the east and west coasts. The following version was collected at the Naval Air Station in Alameda, California, in 1974, and is still in active circulation. For other versions, see YWIW [77], and "Points to Ponder," *Reader's Digest*, 145, no. 869 (September 1994), 161.

> We trained hard.....but it seemed that every time we were beginning to form up into teams we would be reorganized.....I was to learn later in life that we tend to meet any new situation by reorganizing; and a wonderful method it can be for creating the illusion of progress while producing confusion, inefficiency, and demoralization
>
> Petronius Arbiter, 210 BC

15. Tomorrow We've Got to Get Organized

While too much organization can be counterproductive, not enough may be disastrous. The following item from Manchester, England, in 1978, suggests the consequences of insufficient organization.

For other versions of this item, see Gillian Bennett, "'God I Love This Place!' The Workplace as Presented in Photocopied Joke-Sheets: A Visual Essay," in Gillian Bennett, ed., *Spoken in Jest* (Sheffield, England: Sheffield Academic Press, 1991), 196; OG2, [28]; OHB, 32; and RIF, 42.

16. Are You Lonely?

Being a member of an organization requires constant contact and communication with others. While some interaction can be readily accomplished through telephones and electronic media, there remains a feeling that there is really no substitute for face-to-face interchanges. In some organizations, one may come to think that a normal day consists of nothing but a series of endless meetings. The following example offers a pointed commentary on the uselessness of such meetings. The first version was collected in the Wyoming Department of Commerce, in Cheyenne, Wyoming, in November 1994, while the second was found at the Syracuse University Press in 1995. For another version, see OJ2, 329.

ARE YOU LONELY?
TIRED OF WORKING ON YOUR OWN?
DO YOU HATE MAKING DECISIONS?

HOLD A MEETING !!!

YOU CAN...

- ✗ <u>SEE</u> people
- ✗ <u>DRAW</u> org-charts
- ✗ <u>FEEL</u> important
- ✗ <u>IMPRESS</u> your colleagues
- ✗ <u>EAT</u> donuts

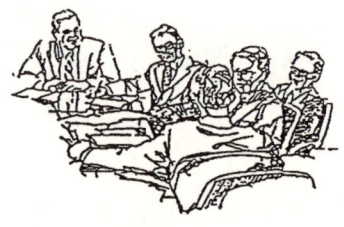

ALL ON COMPANY TIME!!!

MEETINGS
...the practical alternative to work

ARE YOU LONELY?

Hate to work on your own?

Hate to make decisions?

Then, Hold a Meeting!

You can see other people, sleep in peace, off-load decisions, feel important and impress your colleagues.

MEETINGS!
THE PRACTICAL ALTERNATIVE TO WORK

17. There Is No Pleasure

Leisure as a concept is meaningless without the context of work. Having too little work or being unemployed is a much less desirable alternative to being overworked. One cannot enjoy escape unless there is something to escape from. The following item was collected at Hendrix College in Conway, Arkansas in July 1987.

18. I Did It Right the First Time

One must not only work, but one must also give the appearance of working. The following popular item provides a feminist perspective on this principle. It suggests that men look busy because they are inefficient, as opposed to women who don't appear to be busy because they are efficient. The wording in the four versions presented remains fairly constant, but the layout and the accompanying images show considerable variation. The first version is from Savage, Minnesota in 1994; the second from the Bank of Boston in 1993; the third and fourth from San Francisco in 1991 and 1994. For another version, see FOJ, 73.

Of Course I don't look as busy as the men. I did it Right the First Time!

19. The Last Revision

While doing it right the first time is a noble desideratum, it is unfortunately a rarity. Whether one's boss asks for changes or a fickle client requests alterations, a given design may go through many transformations before attaining final acceptance. The following traditional poem was collected in 1977 at a Pacific Gas and Electric Office from an electrical engineer. The cartoon was obtained from an architect in Oakland, California in 1988. For another version of the cartoon, see OHB, 31.

```
The Last Revision

The Draftsmen and The Engineer
   Are Men of Skill and Vision
At Least They Are Until They Hear
   The Hated Word—REVISION

The Engineer With Practiced Eye
   Surveys His Grand Design
The Draftsmen Then Expertly Draws
   Each Complicated Line.

"Complete," They Sigh Contentedly
   "Miraculous Precision"
Oh Optimists! Tomorrow Brings
   Catastrophe! Revision!

Revision One Adds This New Piece
   Revision Two Improves It
Revision Three Makes It Just Right
   Then Number Four Removes It.

"You Can't Do This, You Can't Do That
   "We'll Wait for A Decision"
"But In The Meantime Just Revise
   That Last Revised Revision."

Revise! Revise! The Very Word
   Fills Engineers With Dread
Tho' Die They Must, They'll Be Revised
   To Make Damn Sure They're Dead.

They Hope That God's No Engineer
   When He Makes His Decision
If Once They Win Their Wings, They Hope
   There'll Be No Last REVISION.
```

20. Make One More Change!

In the context of an endless series of requests for revision, it is tempting to wish one could take strong and decisive action to call a halt to these requests. However, to do this would probably require one to buck the system, which might well jeopardize one's job security. The following item expresses this wishful thinking by referring to the Clint Eastwood movie character Inspector Callahan, or Dirty Harry, who was a vigilante who did not hesitate to take matters into his own hands when he felt the justice system of society failed him. In a series of films (Dirty Harry, 1971; Magnum Force, 1973; The Enforcer, 1976) one of the most memorable scenes shows Dirty Harry, who often used guns to make his point, taunting a criminal by daring him to go for his gun and saying "Go Ahead, Make My Day," thereby indicating that he would be happy to shoot him down if he made such a move. That particular scene inspired the following item of photocopier folklore. The three versions presented show variation in format, the type of gun, and the image. Most, but not all, of the images do bear some resemblance to Clint Eastwood. The first version is from Berkeley, California in 1993; the second from Mountain View, California in the late 1980s; and the third is from Chicago in 1994.

GO AHEAD MAKE ONE MORE CHANGE

21. Go Ahead

The ubiquity of guns in the workplace is reflected in the following item inasmuch as it is a woman, not Dirty Harry, who threatens the person she faces. There have been far too many instances of fatal shootings by disgruntled former employees or others in post offices, fast food outlets, schools, law firms, and other commercial or governmental offices. Such tragic incidents have accelerated the efforts to ban assault weapons and to limit or prohibit the indiscriminate purchase or possession of handguns. The first item was collected from a Sacramento, California law office in 1990, while the second came from a San Francisco law office in 1992. For another version, see FOJ2, 295.

22. The Hawaiian Gourmet & Luau Society

Placing one item on someone's desk in an office may be annoying, but it is not intimidating. The following feigned threat collected from a legal secretary in San Francisco in the 1950s is a conglomerate nightmare. For another example of an exaggerated threat, see SD, 351.

> *The Hawaiian Gourmet & Luau Society*
> *takes pleasure in announcing*
> *that you have been honored as the*
> *Official Host for their first visit to the mainland.*
> *15 live pigs, 20 cases of frozen fish, 15 sacks of*
> *dried octopus and squid and 2000 coconuts*
> *will be delivered to your residence within a week.*
> *The Royal cooks, musicians and hula dancers*
> *follow, to be your house guests for a month.*
> *In your honor, the Royal cannon will fire a*
> *salute from your roof daily, at sunrise.*
>
> *The Committee*

23. The Airport Commission Is Pleased to Announce

Threats do not always come from individuals. Sometimes a governmental agency is the source. There is a widespread apprehension about governmental action that may impact upon an individual homeowner's peace and serenity. Highway construction, the licensing of bars or adult book stores, the location of drug rehabilitation centers, and the arbitrary placement of paroled child molesters and other ex-felons are examples of bureaucratic decisions that may engender alarm and protest by concerned citizens. The following item, collected in Northport, New York, in 1996, pretends that the government does not intend to disrupt the addressee's life.

The Airport Commission

Is Pleased To Announce That

The Main Runway

Of The New Jetport Facility

To Be Constructed In Your Area Will Terminate

25 Yards Short Of Your Property.

It Will Therefore Not Be Necessary For Us

To Condemn and Purchase Your House.

You May Continue

To Live In Your Present Location.

24. To Get Along in This World

Two of the most annoying characteristics of business associates or customers are outright stupidity and uncalled-for rudeness. On occasion, both traits may manifest themselves simultaneously. The following rejoinder to such misconduct was collected in Montgomery, Alabama in 1991. The lightbulb frame is undoubtedly intended to illustrate brightness, as a lightbulb is a standard symbol of a good idea or creative brilliance.

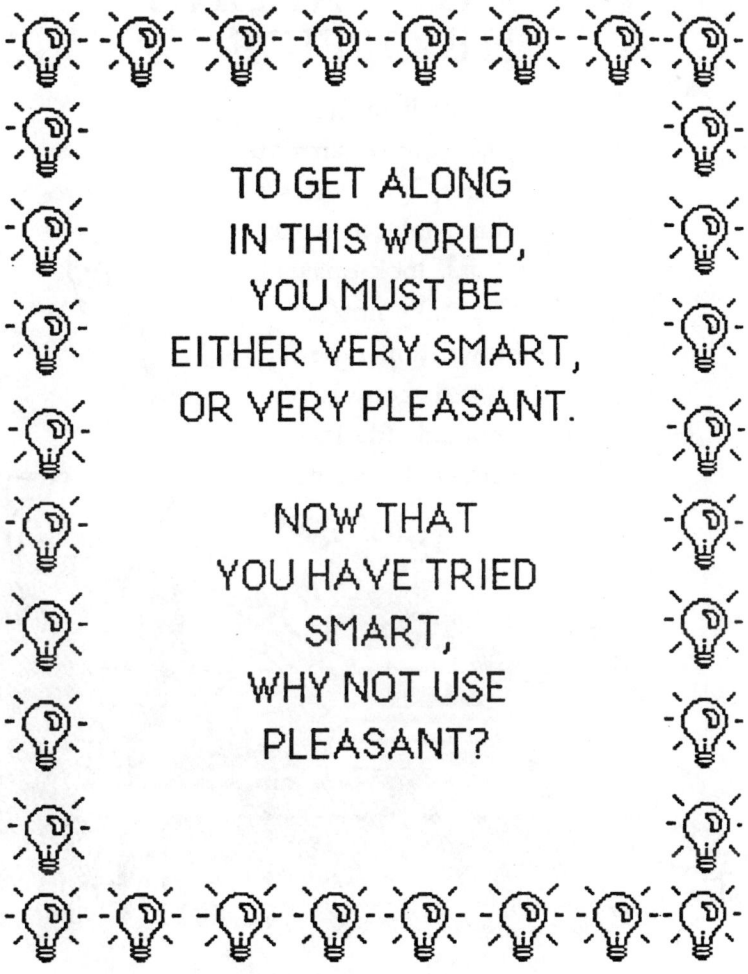

25. How to Get Along at the Office

Customers and clients are not the only sources of annoying behavior in the business world. Incompetent or lazy office workers can be equally frustrating. The following purported list of prescribed procedures itemizes some of the most common complaints about office inefficiency. It was collected at DePauw University in Greencastle, Indiana in 1997. For a version with text only, titled "Secretary's Checklist," see FOJ, 187.

HOW TO GET ALONG AT THE OFFICE

If it rings, put it on hold;
If it clanks, call the repairman;
If it whistles, ignore it;
If it's a friend, take a break;
If it's a boss, look busy;
If it talks, take notes;
If it's handwritten, type it;
If it's typed, copy it;
If it's copied, file it;
If it's Friday, forget it!

26. Lord, Grant Me the Serenity

When one is suddenly confronted with mindless stupidity or obnoxious rudeness, there are two basic alternatives. The first is to vent one's spleen by yelling, cursing, gnashing one's teeth, and the like. Or, instead, one can grin and bear it stoically. With the latter course of action (or inaction), a well-known quotation composed by Protestant theologian and social philosopher Reinhold Niebuhr (1892–1971) may come to mind. The "Serenity Prayer" published in 1934 is as follows:

God, give us grace to accept with serenity the things that cannot be changed, courage to change the things which should be changed, and the wisdom to distinguish the one from the other.

The folk have appropriated Niebuhr's prayer, and in this popular parody, we find that the wording has been altered and the conclusion drastically changed. The folk ending completely eviscerates the fundamental message of the original prayer. The version of this item presented here, collected in Savage, Minnesota in 1994, is somewhat atypical insofar as it is framed by graphic images. Other versions, collected coast to coast, are normally unadorned. For another version, see FOJ2, 397.

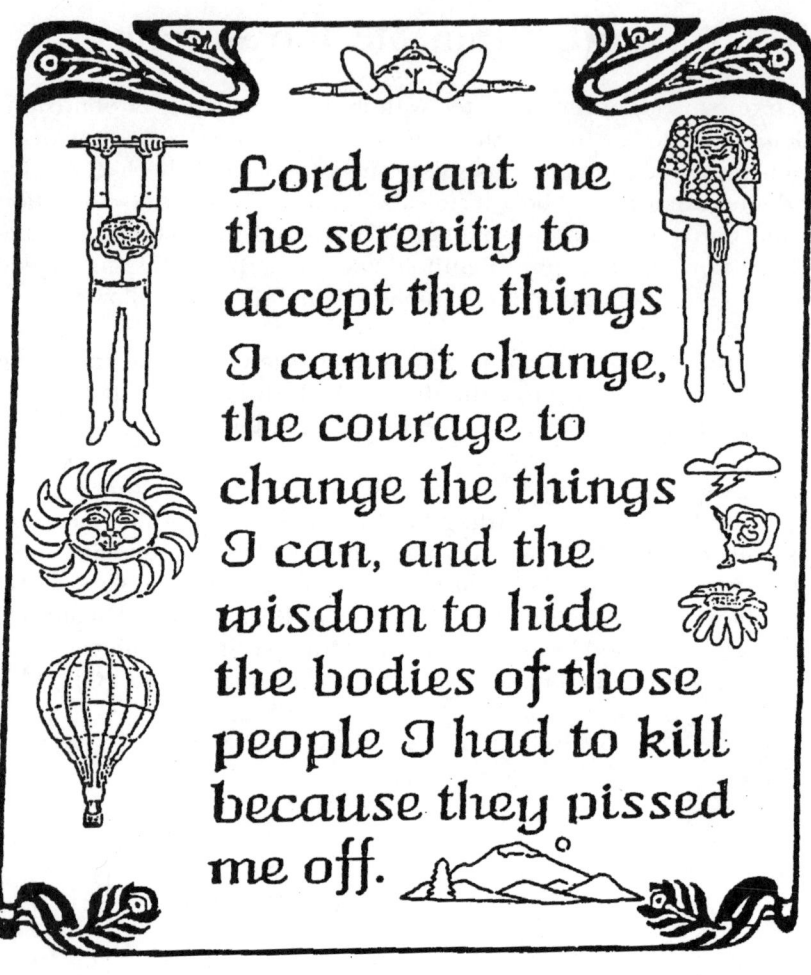

27. Take Care!!!

One reason to refrain from taking action when frustrated is that there may be repercussions from such action. An insulted or aggrieved individual may turn out to be a future superior who may seek to exact retribution. The first version was collected in Berkeley, California in 1994. The second, collected in Stockton, California, in 1996, titled "Office Prayer" combines this item with the Serenity Prayer parody. Just as two distinct tale types can occasionally combine, and just as two separate folksongs may merge, so also diverse photocopier traditions can coalesce.

> **TAKE CARE !!!**
> The toes you step on today could be connected to the ass you have to kiss tomorrow.

Office Prayer

Grant me the serenity

To accept the things I cannot change,

The courage

To change the things I cannot accept,

And the wisdom

To hide the bodies of those people I had

to kill today because they pissed me off.

Also,

Help me to be careful

Of the toes I step on today, as they

May be connected to the ass

That I might have to kiss tomorrow.

28. There Is No Evidence

Stepping on toes does not have to be literal. One can step on toes by saying something inappropriate, foolish, or insulting. The following text was collected in Iselin, New Jersey in 1992.

"There is no evidence that the tongue is connected to the brain."

29. Quality Is Like Buying Oats

Part of a salesman's job is quoting prices to prospective customers. Customers always want to know the lowest possible price. Typically, there is a considerable difference between the cost of new and used items. The following text serves as an effective reminder that one gets what one pays for. The first version, a photocopy of a wall plaque, was collected in Virginia in 1976, while the second was collected in Northport, New York in mid-1996. A wallet card version (not presented here), with a text similar to the first version, circulated in Wilmington, Delaware in 1956. For another version, see FOJ2, 269.

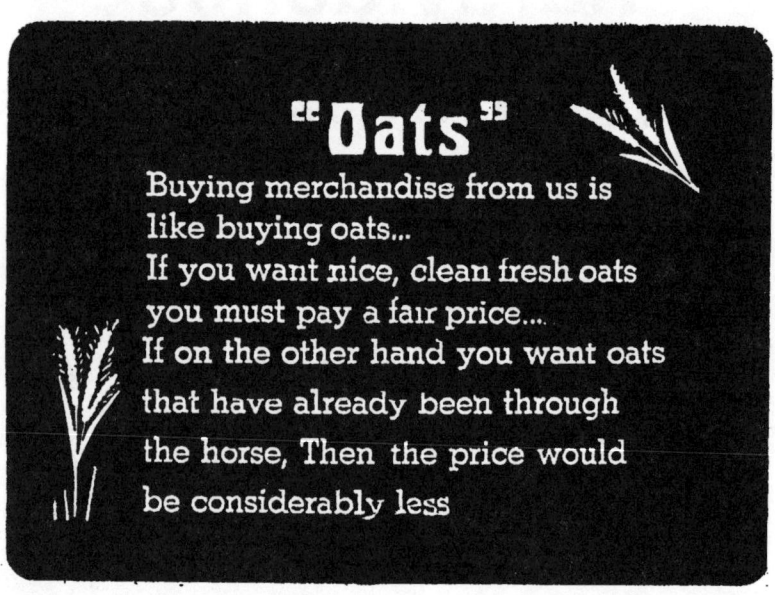

"Oats"
Buying merchandise from us is like buying oats...
If you want nice, clean fresh oats you must pay a fair price...
If on the other hand you want oats that have already been through the horse, Then the price would be considerably less

30. Can You Make This Thing Work?

The rapid rate of technological change makes it difficult for some older corporate managers to keep pace with innovations in office equipment. Chief Executive Officers (CEOs) have accordingly become increasingly dependent upon specially trained subordinates to carry out basic tasks. The following item was reported in San Francisco in January 1997. It is a sad commentary on this situation.

A young executive was leaving the office at 6 p.m. when he found the CEO standing in front of a shredder with a piece of paper in hand.

"Listen," said the CEO, "this is important, and my secretary has left. Can you make this thing work?"

"Certainly," said the young executive. He turned the machine on, inserted the paper, and pressed the start button.

"Excellent, excellent!" said the CEO as his paper disappeared inside the machine. "I just need one copy."

31. No Machine Can Do My Job

One of the legitimate fears of modern workers is that automation may eliminate their jobs. As technology has advanced, machines, including the computer, have become ever more efficient. Some workers feel that they have had to become more like machines to survive. By the same token, workers have also sought to humanize machines, e.g., by giving them names. The following versions collected in the San Francisco Bay area in 1977 and late 1980s reflect both these tendencies. Presumably machines are not yet sufficiently humanized to need or enjoy alcohol.

32. Notice to All Employees

The pressure of making a living can drive a person to drink. Alcoholism is a major social problem in the United States and elsewhere, and it occurs not infrequently in the business world. Social drinking, in fact, is sometimes a virtual necessity for employees charged with entertaining clients or visiting members of the firm. The following folk commentary from Northport, New York, in 1996, spells out the problem. We have intentionally left the misspelling of "liqueur" and "employees" as they appear in that form on some versions dating back to 1977. For other versions, see UFFC-TB, 39, and FOJ2, 296.

NOTICE TO ALL EMPLOYES

Nobody minds a man having a morning eye-opener and it's O.K. to have a bracer around 10 a.m. and a couple of drinks before lunch. And a few beers on a hot afternoon to keep a man healthy or at least happy. And, of course everyone drinks at a cocktail hour. And a man can't be criticized for having wine with his dinner, a liquor afterwards and a highball or two during the evening — but this damn business of SIP, SIP, SIP, all day long HAS GOT TO STOP!

33. Happiness Is...

If a person is discontented with his or her boss, that person may either quit, or hope that the boss leaves. The following item was collected at Goucher College in Baltimore, Maryland in 1993. The practice of putting pictures of missing children on milk cartons (as a means of encouraging the public to report any traces of these children) provides the basis for a presumably disgruntled employee's wishful thinking. The "Happiness Is..." formula is a standard cliché for saccharine platitudes. For a version with the text only, see FOJ, 89; for another parodic example employing this formula, see NT, 385.

Happiness is ---
waking up in the
morning and finding
a picture of your
boss on the milk
carton

34. Doing a Good Job Here

One reason for being unhappy with one's boss is the feeling of being unappreciated. An extreme expression of discontent suggests that not only is good work unrecognized and unrewarded, but that it, in fact, seems to lead to disagreeable consequences. In one of the most popular pieces of photocopier folklore, several of Charles Schulz's celebrated cartoon characters are pressed into folk service.

The dozens of versions appear to fall into two major subtypes. The first involves an analogy to working in a whorehouse; the second to wetting one's pants. These earthy themes are in marked contrast to the basically wholesome nature of the Peanuts comic strip. With respect to the latter assessment, some individuals have even gone so far as to perceive Peanuts adventures as Christian allegory. See, for example, Robert L. Short, *The Gospel According to Peanuts* (Richmond: John Knox Press, 1965) and the same author's *The Parables of Peanuts* (New York: Harper and Row, 1968). For other photocopier treatments of Peanuts characters, see WY, 109, 175–77; WH 185–88; NT, 359.

The first subtype is represented by four versions: from New York City in 1991, Iselin, New Jersey, in 1989, Montgomery, Alabama, in 1991, and the San Francisco Bay Area in the 1980s. The second subtype is presented in three versions: from Oakland in the late 1970s, Montgomery, Alabama, in 1991, and Oakland in 1980. Although the wording of both subtypes remains fairly stable, the associated cartoon elements reveal considerable variation. For other versions of the first subtype, see Gillian Bennett, " 'God I Love This Place!' The Workplace as Presented in Photocopied Joke-Sheets: A Visual Essay," in Gillian Bennett, ed., *Spoken in Jest* (Sheffield, England: Sheffield Academic Press, 1991), 186; FOJ, 39, OHB, 24, RIF, 37, YD, 165, YWIW, 101.

35. This Job Is a Test

Another form of protest against the lack of rewards for superior job performance parodies the standard emergency radio broadcast signal. The signal consists of a long monotonous tone followed by a voice message explaining that there is no actual crisis, but that if there had been, listeners would have been instructed as to what action to take. The implication of this parody is that the job in question is only an exercise and not a real job. For another parody of the same emergency procedure, see NT, 118. The following text was reported in Oakland in 1994.

**This job is a test.
It is only a Test.
Had this been an actual job, you would have received raises, promotions and other signs of appreciation.**

36. Enjoy Life

Whatever the difficulties one may encounter on the job or elsewhere, there is something to be said for appreciating and taking advantage of as many of life's opportunities as possible. From a purely hedonistic perspective, one should probably not postpone pleasure in the hopes of a better existence in the next world. This life may be all there is, and if so, time and existence are precious. The folk say all this much better in the following item collected from the laboratory at the Pacific Presbyterian Medical Center in San Francisco in 1994.

37. If You Have to Walk on Thin Ice

Living life to the fullest may be a worthwhile philosophy, but some may urge caution in view of the multitude of potential perils. On the other hand, an excess of caution may result in many lost possibilities for enjoyment. In such cases, a fatalist might choose to throw caution to the winds. Adopting the perspective contained in the Biblical "Eat, Drink, and Be Merry for Tomorrow We Shall Die" (Isaiah 22:13) would support a course of action ignoring signs of danger. The following item was collected in Oakland, California in 1979.

if you have to walk on thin ice, you might as well dance.

38. Thank You and Goodbye

One of the dangers in life involves con games and scams that may wrongfully fleece a gullible public. Previously reliable financial institutions, e.g., savings and loan associations, may fail; real estate investments may sour; and businesses of any type may disappear through mergers or be dissolved for other reasons. In such cases, the consumer may have little or no recourse. The following item parodies the form letter sent to such consumers. It was collected in Detroit in 1983.

Inasmuch as we handle your checking

and savings accounts

we are taking this opportunity to inform you

of our unexpected change of address.

By the time of your receipt of this notice

our move will have been effected.

Thank you, and goodbye.

39. Remember Me?

If a business continues to exist, an aggrieved consumer always has the option of 1) writing a strong letter of complaint, and 2) no longer patronizing the business in question. The following item was collected in Oakland, California in 1992.

REMEMBER ME?

I'm the fellow who goes into a restaurant, sits down patiently, and waits while the waitresses do everything but take my order.

I'm the fellow who goes into a department store, and stands quietly while the sales clerks finish their chit chat.

I'm the man who goes into a reception room, on time for a business appointment, and stands by the desk while the receptionist finishes her personal telephone call.

I'm the fellow who never comes back, and it amuses me to see you spending money every year to try to get me back to your company, when I was there in the first place, and all you had to do to keep me was to show me a little courtesy.

Wordplay

Language can be a rich source of humor. Puns and other forms of verbal wit are commonplace in photocopier folklore. The items in this chapter reveal a broad spectrum of linguistic creativity. Types of material include lists, euphemisms, paradoxes, and parodies of advertising slogans, among others.

40. Clinton Deploys Vowels to Bosnia

With the breakup of the former country of Yugoslavia, the various repressed ethnic enclaves sought independence. However, the Serbian majority resisted such attempts and tried to maintain dominance over such groups. One of the most extreme examples of this occurred in Bosnia, where a bitter civil war erupted between Christian Serbs and a large Moslem community, the situation complicated further by Croats, who had their own longstanding rivalry with the Serbs. The ethnic animosities in the Balkans are centuries old. Attempts at so-called ethnic cleansing resulted in countless bloody massacres and brutal executions of women and children, reported in all-too-gory detail by the media.

Appalled by such genocidal mayhem, the United States and its Western European allies wanted to intervene. After exhausting fruitless diplomatic efforts, a United Nations peacekeeping force somewhat reluctantly was sent to stabilize Bosnia. The force included an American component. It was a difficult decision for an American president to make. Placing young American men and women in harm's way to impose a precarious peace in a highly volatile situation did not please everyone.

The following parody of the presidential decision is couched in linguistic terms. From an American ethnocentric perspective, Bosnian personal and place names seem hard to spell or pronounce. In this context, the Bosnians are depicted as being dissatisfied with their own language and as welcoming the American aid. It was collected in Berkeley, California in 1996.

January 30, 1996

WORLD NEWS:

CLINTON DEPLOYS VOWELS TO BOSNIA

Cities of Sjlbdvdnzv, Grsvy to Be First Recipients

Before an emergency joint session of Congress yesterday, President Clinton announced US plans to deploy over 75,000 vowels to the war-torn region of Bosnia. The deployment, the largest of its kind in American history, will provide the region with the critically needed letters A, E, I, O and U, and is hoped to render countless Bosnian names more pronounceable.

"For six years, we have stood by while names like Ygrqvslhv and Tzlynhr and Glrm have been horribly butchered by millions around the world," Clinton said. "Today, the United States must finally stand up and say, 'Enough.' It is time the people of Bosnia finally had some vowels in their incomprehensible words. The US is proud to lead the crusade in this noble endeavor."

The deployment, dubbed Operation Vowel Movement by the State Department, is set for early next week, with the Adriatic port cities of Sjlbvdnzv and Grzny slated to be the first recipients. Two C-130 transport planes, each carrying over 500 24-count boxes of "E's," will fly from Andrews Air Force Base across the Atlantic and airdrop the letters over the cities.

Citizens of Grzny and Sqlbvdnzv eagerly awaited the arrival of the vowels. "My God, I do not think we can last another day," Trszg Grzdnjkln, 44, said. "I have six children and none of them has a name that is understandable to me or to anyone else. Mr. Clinton, please send my poor, wretched family just one 'E.' Please." Said Sjlbvdnzv resident Grg Hmphrs, 67: "With just a few key letters, I could be George Humphries. This is my dream."

If the initial airlift is successful, Clinton said the United States will go ahead with full-scale vowel deployment, with the C-130's airdropping thousands more letters over every area of Bosnia. Other nations are expected to pitch in as well, including 10,000 British "A's" and 6,500 Canadian "U's." Japan, rich in A's and O's, was asked to participate, but declined.

"With these valuable letters, the people of war-ravaged Bosnia will be able to make some terrific new words," Clinton said. "It should be very exciting for them, and much easier for us to read their maps."

Linguists praise the US's decision to send the vowels. For decades they have struggled with the hard consonants and difficult pronunciation of most Slavic words. "Vowels are crucial to construction of all languages," Baylor University linguist Nome Frankel said. "Without them, it would be difficult to utter a single word, much less organize a coherent sentence. Please, just don't get me started on the moon-man languages they use in those Eastern European countries." According to Frankel, once the Bosnians have vowels, they will be able to construct such sentences as: "The potatoes are ready"; "I believe it will rain"; and "Oh, my God, there's an axe in my head."

The airdrop represents the largest deployment of any letter to a foreign country since 1984. During the summer of that year, the US shipped 92,000 consonants to Ethiopia, providing cities like Auaouuoaua, Eaoiiuae, and Aao with vital, life-giving supplies of L's, S's and T's. The consonant-relief effort failed, however, when vast quantities of the letters were intercepted and hoarded by violent, gun-toting warlords.

41. Who Makxs a Group a Succxss?

Of all the vowels in the English language, perhaps the most common is represented orthographically by the letter "E." The difficulty of trying to get along without it is effectively illustrated in the following text collected in a sorority house on the Berkeley campus in 1994. The American stress on "rugged individualism" with the associated notion that every individual has value and that no group can function efficiently without every single person contributing is also featured.

WHO MAKXS A GROUP A SUCCXSS?

Xvxn though my typxwritxr is an old modxl, it still works quitx wxll xxcxpt for onx kxy. I havx wishxd many timxs that it workxd pxrfxctly. It is trux that thxrx arx 41 othxr kxys that do function wxll xnough, but just onx not working makxs all thx diffxrxncx. Somxtimxs it sxxms to mx that our group is somxwhat likx an old typxwritxr–not all of thx lxttxrs arx working propxrly. You may say to yoursxlf, "Wxll, I am only onx pxrson. I won't makx or brxak an organization." But, it doxs makx a diffxrxncx bxcausx for a group to bx xffxctivx it nxxds activx participation of xvxry singlx pxrson. So, thx nxxt timx you think you arx only onx pxrson, and that your xfforts arx not nxxdxd, rxmxmbxr my old typxwritxr and say to yourslef, "I am a kxy pxrson in this group and I am nxxded vxry much."

42. You Foul-Mouthed Swine

One source of verbal humor comes from the use of dialect. Most American immigrant groups have jokes that play on mispronunciations or misunderstandings of standard English. At the same time, these groups themselves are not infrequently depicted in stereotypic terms as speaking with a strong accent, e.g., Irish, German, Scandinavian, and others. The following joke, collected in Berkeley via e-mail in 1996, depends upon a pseudo-Italian accent as well as an extended double entendre. Another version (not presented here), collected in San Francisco in late 1996, is titled "Eye-Ties." For another version, see Larry Wilde, *The Official Wilde and Dirty Joke Book* (New York: Pinnacle Books, 1985), 40. For other photocopier folklore involving Italian-American accents, see WH, 129, WY, 39–40, 253–54, SC 124–25; for double entendres, see WH, 196–219, WY, 215–33.

A bus stops and two Italian men get on. They seat themselves and engage in an animated conversation. The lady sitting behind them ignores their conversation at first, but she listens in horror as one of the men says the following:

"Emma come first. Den I come. Two asses, dey come together. I come again. Two asses, dey come together again. I come again and pee twice. Den I come once-a-more!"

"You foul mouthed swine!" exclaims the lady indignantly. "In this country we do not talk about our sex lives in public!!!"

"Hey coola down lady," said the man. "Imma just tellun my friend how to spell Mississippi!"

The name Mississippi has also inspired other folklore. For example, one traditional way of spelling this word, a mnemonic device, is: M I crooked letter, crooked letter I, Crooked letter, crooked letter I, Humpback, humpback I. One of the authors learned this from his father in New York State in the late 1940s and it was reported in Santa Cruz, California in the early 1980s.

43. Welcome to the Psychiatric Hot Line

Technology has revolutionized daily life and, in theory, it promotes efficiency. In practice, it may actually prove to be more frustrating than useful. A case in point is the escalating employment of automated telephone answering machines. Many companies, tired of answering the same questions again and again, day after day, have devised recorded responses that supposedly cover all eventualities. The caller must first listen to a long, long laundry list of options after which he or she must select one or more to get a question answered. With this system in place, it becomes almost impossible to speak to a living human being.

Moreover, sometimes the particular question for which one is seeking an answer is not even one of the possible options, but in any case, the caller is obliged to listen all the way through the lengthy litany to discover this fact.

In the following text collected in San Francisco in June 1997, we find a clever critique of the idea that complex problems can be solved instantaneously with one simple phone call or by pushing one single button.

Welcome to the Psychiatric Hotline

If you are obsessive-compulsive:

>Please press 1 repeatedly.

If you are co-dependent:

>Please ask someone to press 2.

If you have multiple personalities:

>Please press 3, 4, 5, and 6.

If you are paranoid-delusional:

>We know who you are and what you want. Just stay on the line so we can trace the call.

If you are schizophrenic:

>Listen carefully ... a little voice will tell you which number to press.

If you are manic-depressive:

>It doesn't matter which number you press; no one will answer.

44. Word Association

One of the techniques developed in psychiatry as an initial diagnostic tool is a form of word association test. Supposedly, a patient's free association to a word (or a dream symbol) provides the analyst with a clue as to the patient's mental problem. C. G. Jung, the founder of analytical psychology, carried out important research on word association tests early in his career. See C. G. Jung, *Studies in Word-Association* (London: Heinemann, 1918). For other considerations of this important technique, see Phebe Cramer, *Word Association* (New York: Academic Press, 1968); and Leo Postman and Geoffrey Keppel, eds., *Norms of Word Association* (New York: Academic Press, 1970).

The following text was collected in Berkeley via a Fax from Phoenix, Arizona in May of 1994. (For another text playing upon bird names including swallow, see RDJ, 553).

Word Association

Bold and Daring:	What kind of bird do you think of?	Answer: Eagle
Knowledgeable:	What kind of bird do you think of?	Answer: Owl
In Love:	What kind of bird do you think of?	Answer: Dove
Really In love!!!:	What kind of bird do you think of?	Answer: Swallow!!!

45. Straight Man Test

Homophobia exists in the United States and elsewhere, a fact that makes it difficult for gay males to openly profess their sexual preference. One of the commonly articulated fears of straight males is that they might be accused (wrongly or rightly) of having homosexual tendencies. The following mock-test, collected from an electronic bulletin board at a computer company in Mountain View, California, in 1991, plays on this fear. The explicit allusion to a possible homoerotic component in American football confirms a theory to that end. For an initial statement of the theory, see Alan Dundes, "Into the Endzone for a Touchdown: A Psychoanalytic Consideration of American Football," *Western Folklore* 37 (1978), 75–88. For a refinement and extension of the theory, see the title essay in Alan Dundes, *From Game to War and Other Psychoanalytic Essays on Folklore* (Lexington: Univ. Press of Kentucky, 1997). We have retained the double entry for question eight on the test in accordance with our policy of not correcting or altering texts.

The following is the Straight Man test—score 10 points for each correct answer.

---

1. What does a straight man call it when his wife won't put out and he can't get any anywhere?

Traditional values.

2. What does a straight man call it when his wife won't put out, he can't get any anywhere, his baby keeps him awake all night, his five-year-old throws up on him and his ten-year-old totals the family car?

Family values.

3. What does a straight man call it when two straight men hug, kiss, and fondle each others buttocks?

Football.

4. What does a straight man do when the urge to "play football" becomes irresistible?

Posts homophobic jokes to the net.

5. What do you call a straight man with absolutely no taste in music, literature, art or cinema?

Typical.

6. What do you call a straight man who can walk without tripping over his feet?

Graceful.

7. Why can't straight men play the piano?

They think the black keys are unnatural.

8. What does a straight man call another straight man with good taste who can walk without tripping over his feet and can play the piano?

A fag.

8. What do you call a straight man who likes more kinds of sex than the missionary position?

A pervert.

9. What do you call a straight man who likes getting a blow job?

Sexually frustrated.

10. What do you call it when a straight man asks a woman out in the most suave, sophisticated manner of which he is capable?

Sexual harassment.

46. T-Shirts in Castro Street Shops

San Francisco is a city known to be hospitable to and tolerant of homosexuals. One of the districts largely associated with this group is called the "Castro" after Castro Street. There are oral jokes that refer specifically to this area. For example, "If you drop a quarter on Castro Street, don't pick it up until it rolls to Van Ness [Street]." In another version, "If you drop a quarter on Castro, kick it to Van Ness before you bend over to pick it up." Other jokes referring to the large homosexual presence in San Francisco include: "What's the longest bridge in the world? Answer: The Bay Bridge ... It runs all the way from Africa [Oakland] to Fairyland."

The following purported list of T-shirt slogans was collected in San Francisco in early 1994. For explanations of homosexual slang, see Bruce Rodgers, *The Queen's Vernacular* (San Francisco: Straight Arrow Books, 1972), reprinted as *Gaytalk* (New York: Paragon, 1979). For general American homosexual folklore, see Joseph P. Goodwin, *More Man Than You'll Ever Be: Gay Folklore and Acculturation in Middle America* (Bloomington: Indiana Univ. Press, 1989).

```
T-SHIRTS IN CASTRO STREET SHOPS

Queen Without A Country

I Can't Even Think Straight

It Happens In The Best Of Families

Hate Is Not A Family Value

Life Is Hard, Then You Nap

I Don't Mind Straight People As Long As They Act Gay In Public

He's Out Of Town ...

I'm Not Getting Older; I'm Getting Bitter

And Now For My Next Trick

Sorry Mom, No Grandkids

Recycle -- Sleep With An Ex

One Percent?  Did Anyone Check The Closets?

Breakfast Included

Pink Trash

The Family Tree Stops Here

Don't Knock Masturbation; It's Sex With Someone I Love
```

47. Country Songs

One category of American popular music is "Country and Western," often termed simply "Country." It began in the white rural south centered particularly around Nashville, Tennessee. (For a historical review of country music and its growth, see Bill C. Malone, *Country Music, U.S.A.* (Austin: Univ. of Texas Press, 1968). See also Barry McCloud, *Definitive Country: The Ultimate Encyclopedia of Country Music and Its Performers* (New York: Berkeley Publishing Group, 1995). The lyrics of many country songs are sentimental earthy laments about lost loves, infidelity, alcoholism, and other examples of life's misfortunes. Song writers in this genre often signal the dramatic content of their compositions by choosing a striking, novel phrase that typically recurs in the refrain. To the uninitiated, some of the country song titles might seem excessively maudlin or amusingly frivolous. The following item, collected in Berkeley in 1993, parodies this aspect of such songs. For another version, see *The Best of Uncle John's Bathroom Reader* (Ashland, Oregon: Bathroom Reader's Press, 1995), 433.

Another version (not presented here) from San Francisco in 1996, titled "The Best of the Worst Country-Western Song Titles" contained the following additional titles:

"Get Your Tongue Outta My Mouth 'Cause I'm Kissing You Goodbye"

"I Can't Get Over You, So Why Don't You Get Under Me?'

"I Don't Know Whether to Come Home or Go Crazy"

"I Don't Know Whether to Kill Myself or Go Bowling"

"I Hate Every Bone in Your Body Except Mine"

"I Knew I'd Hit Rock Bottom When I Woke Up on Top of Ewe"

"I Still Miss You Baby, But My Aim's Gettin' Better"

"I Wish I Were in Dixie Tonight, But She's Out of Town"

"If I Had Shot You When I Wanted To, I'd Be Out By Now"

COUNTRY SONGS

"Don't cry on my shoulders 'cause you're rusting my spurs."

"How can I miss you if you won't go away?"

"I can't love your body if your heart's not in it."

"I fell in a pile of you, and got love all over me."

"I would have writ you a letter, but I couldn't spell 'yeech!'"

"I wouldn't take her to a dawg fight, 'cause I'm afraid she'd win."

"I'm so miserable without you, it's like having you here."

"If I can't be No. 1 in your life, then No. 2 on you."

"If you don't leave me alone, I'll go and find someone else who will."

"My everyday silver is plastic."

"I'll get over you, as soon as you get out from under him."

"My wife ran off with my best friend, and I sure do miss him."

"They may put me in prison, but they can't stop my face from breaking out."

"You're the reason our baby's so ugly."

48. I Love Country Music

Country music, like other American popular musics, has its own devoted set of fans. The following rebus articulates a slogan that also appears as a bumper sticker. It was collected in San Jose, California in November 1995. For other examples of photocopier rebus items, see WY 136–41; SD 98–99.

49. Reasons Why E-Mail Is Like a Penis

E[lectronic]-Mail not only transmits photocopier folklore, but it has become itself the subject of such folklore. The following text was collected at Lafayette College in Easton, Pennsylvania in March 1995.

REASONS WHY E-MAIL IS LIKE A PENIS:

Some folks have it, some don't. Those who have it would be devastated if it were ever cut off. They think that those who don't have it are somehow inferior. They think it gives them power. They are wrong. Those who don't have it may agree that it's a nifty toy, but think it's not worth the fuss that those who do have it make about it. Still, many of those who don't have it would like to try it.

It can be up or down. It's more fun when it's up, but it makes it hard to get any real work done.

In the long-distant past, its only purpose was to transmit information considered vital to the survival of the species. Some people still think that's the only thing it should be used for, but most folks today use it for fun most of the time.

Once you've started playing with it, it's hard to stop. Some people would just play with it all day if they didn't have work to do.

It provides a way to interact with other people. Some people take this interaction very seriously, others treat it as a lark. Sometimes it's hard to tell what kind of person you're dealing with until it's too late.

If you don't apply the appropriate protective measures, it can spread viruses.

It has no brain of its own. Instead, it uses yours. If you use it too much, you'll find it becomes more and more difficult to think coherently.

We attach an importance to it that is far greater than its actual size and influence warrant.

If you're not careful what you do with it, it can get you in big trouble.

It has its own agenda. Somehow, no matter how good your intentions, it will warp your behavior. Later you may ask yourself "why on earth did I do that?"

It has no conscience and no memory. Left to its own devices, it will just do the same damn dumb things it did before.

50. 3 Kinds of Sex

It is commonly believed that sexual ardor or passion declines with increasing age. The supposed diminished capacity may, according to the stereotype, result in a total lack of sexuality among the elderly. The following item was collected in Mountain View, California in the late 1980s. For another version, see FOJ2, 440.

3 KINDS OF SEX

HOUSE SEX: WHEN YOU'RE NEWLY MARRIED AND HAVE SEX ALL OVER THE HOUSE, IN EVERY ROOM.

BEDROOM SEX: AFTER YOU'VE BEEN MARRIED FOR A WHILE, YOU JUST HAVE SEX IN THE BEDROOM.

HALL SEX: AFTER YOU'VE BEEN MARRIED FOR MANY, MANY YEARS, YOU JUST PASS EACH OTHER IN THE HALL AND SAY, "FUCK YOU."

51. Four Things That Resemble...

The folk penchant for listing items in series tends to favor the number three in American culture (see Alan Dundes, "The Number Three in American Culture," in Dundes, *Interpreting Folklore* (Bloomington: Indiana Univ. Press, 1980), 134–59). However, there are also traditional sets involving four, five, and other numbers. The following item from ISR dating from the 1950s, and which is probably older, is an example of a *blason populaire*. This French term is preferable to *ethnic slur* inasmuch as many traditional slurs refer to religious groups (e.g., Catholics, Jews, etc.) or to occupational groups (e.g., lawyers, doctors), and to any other folk group. For a discussion of *blason populaire*, see Henri Gaidoz and Paul Sebillot, *Blason Populaire de la France* (Paris: Librarie Leopold Cerf, 1884) and A. A. Roback, *A Dictionary of International Slurs* (Cambridge: Sci-Art Publishers, 1944). The following item caricatures the Irish and Germans.

> FOUR THINGS THAT RESEMBLE AN IRISHMAN
> A monkey, a parrot, a whisky keg and a cow-yard
> A monkey in some respects resembles a human being—
>   So does an Irishman.
> A parrot talks, but has no brains—
>   Same as an Irishman.
> A whisky keg is generally full of whisky—
>   So is an Irishman.
> A cow-yard is a conglomeration of bullshit—
>   So is an Irishman.
>
> FOUR THINGS THAT RESEMBLE A GERMAN
> A flea, a fart, a fly and a ham.
> A flea never turns its back on anyone—
>   Neither does a German.
> A fart never cares to return to its native land—
>   Neither does a German.
> A fly is always in somebody's business but its own—
>   So is a German.
> A ham is not a dam bit of good until it has been hung—
>   Neither is a German.

52. Five Reasons Why It's a Bummer To Be an Egg

A popular sexual double entendre metaphor involves a chicken and an egg. The following two versions of an item illustrate this metaphor. The first was collected in Berkeley in 1987; the second in Los Altos, California in 1994. (For another chicken/egg item, see WH, 157–59.)

FIVE REASONS WHY IT'S A BUMMER

TO BE AN EGG

1. You only get laid once.
2. You only get eaten once.
3. It takes seven minutes to get hard.
4. You have to come in a box with 11 others.
5. The only one who will sit on your face is your mother.

THOUGHT FOR THE DAY

So, you think your life is bad?

Just think how bad the life of an egg is.

You only get laid once.

You only get eaten once.

It takes 4 minutes to get hard, and 2 minutes to get soft.

You have to share a box with 11 other guys,

and the only chick that sits on your face is your mother!!

Now, don't you feel better?

53. A Short Course in Human Relations

Courtesy is something thought to be absent in modern society. Interaction is too often between strangers in a hurry, and the resultant behavior is abrasive and rude. The following item from Walnut Creek, California, in 1988, collected coast to coast, offers a succinct prescription for politeness.

<u>A SHORT COURSE IN HUMAN RELATIONS</u>

The 6 most important words

"I admit I made a mistake."

The 5 most important words

"You did a good job."

The 4 most important words

"What is your opinion?"

The 3 most important words

"If you please."

The 2 most important words

"Thank you."

The 1 most important word

"We"

The LEAST important word . . . . . . "I"

54. Seven Reasons Why Chicago Is Quiet on Sundays

Blason populaire can refer to a single group, but there are also multigroup traditions that consist of numerous ethnic stereotypes contained in a single text. The following item was collected in Chicago in 1994, which is appropriate since there are some local allusions, e.g., to Skokie, a predominantly Jewish community in the metropolitan area.

SEVEN REASONS WHY CHICAGO IS QUIET ON SUNDAYS

1. The Jews are all visiting relatives in Skokie.

2. The Italians are putting flowers on graves.

3. The Irish are all sleeping off hangovers.

4. The Blacks are all in jail.

5. The Puerto Ricans can't get their cars started.

6. The Mexicans are all in the custody of the Immigration Department.

7. The Polacks think it's Tuesday.

55. The Last 10 Things

Stereotypes refer to gender as well as to ethnic groups. Males hold stereotypes of females; females hold stereotypes of males. The following item collected in Berkeley in 1996 provides a comparison of such stereotypes. A second version was collected in San Francisco in 1998; a third also in San Francisco in 1999.

THE LAST TEN THINGS A WOMAN WOULD EVER SAY

10. Could our relationship be more physical? I'm tired of just being friends.
9. Go ahead and leave the seat up. It's easier for me to douche that way.
8. I think hairy backs are really sexy.
7. Does this make my butt look too small?
6. Please don't throw that old T-shirt away. The holes in the armpit are just too cute.
5. This diamond is *way* too big.
4. I won't even put my lips on that thing unless I get to swallow.
3. Wow! It really is 14 inches!
2. You know, I think you should get a girlfriend on the side.
1. I'm wrong. You must be right again.

THE LAST TEN THINGS A MAN WOULD EVER SAY

10. Sometimes I just want to be held.
9. While I'm up, can I get you a strawberry-banana dacqueri?
8. I think hairy legs are really sexy.
7. I think Barry Manilow is one cool guy.
6. I think your driving is excellent.
5. Her breasts are *way* too big.
4. Sure, I'd love to wear a condom.
3. We haven't been to the mall for ages. Let's go shopping together.
2. Fuck Monday Night Football. Let's watch "Murphy Brown."
1. I think we're lost. I'd better pull over and ask directions.

> > >Subject: FW: Eight Things Men/Women never say
> > >
> > >Eight things you'll never hear a man say :
> > >~~~~~~~~~~~~~~~~~~~~~~~~~~~~~~~~~~~~
> > >
> > >8.   Here honey, you use the remote.

> > >
> > >7.   You know, I'd like to see her again, but her breasts are just
> too
> > >big.
> > >
> > >6.   Ooh, Antonio Banderas AND Brad Pitt? That's one movie I gotta
> > see!
> > >
> > >5.   While I'm up, can I get you anything?
> > >
> > >4.   Sex isn't that important, sometimes I just want to be held.
> > >
> > >3.   Aww, forget Monday night football, let's watch Melrose Place.
> > >
> > >2.   Hey, let me hold your purse while you try that on.
> > >
> > >1.   We never talk anymore.
> > >
> > >Eight things you'll never hear a woman say :
> > >~~~~~~~~~~~~~~~~~~~~~~~~~~~~~~~~~~~~
> > >8.   What do you mean today's our anniversary?
> > >
> > >7.   Can we not talk to each other tonight? I'd rather just watch
> TV.
> > >
> > >6.   Ohhhhhh, this diamond is wayyyyyyyyy tooooooo big!
> > >
> > >5.   Can our relationship get a little more physical? I'm tired of
> > being
> > >'just friends'
> > >
> > >4.   Honey, does this outfit make my butt look too small?
> > >
> > >3.   Aww, don't stop for directions, I'm sure you'll be able to
> figure
> > >out how to get there.
> > >
> > >2.   I don't care if it's on sale, $300 is way to much for a
> designer
> > >dress.
> > >
> > >1.   Hey, pull my finger!
> >

> > THINGS A WIFE JUST WON'T SAY
> >
> > 1. I'll swallow it all . . . I love the taste.
> > 2. Are you sure you've had enough to drink?
> > 3. I'm bored. Let's shave my privates!
> > 4. Shouldn't you be down at the bar with your buddies?
> > 5. That was a great fart! Do another one!
> > 6. I've decided to stop wearing clothes around the house.
> > 7. You're so sexy when you're hungover.
> > 8. I'd rather watch football and drink beer with you than go
> > shopping.
> > 9. Let's subscribe to Hustler.
> > 10. Would you like to watch me go down on my girlfriend?
> > 11. Say, let's go down to the mall so you can check out women's
> > asses.
> > 12. I'll be out painting the house.
> > 13. I love it when you play golf on Sunday's, I just wish you had
> > time to play on Saturday too.
> > 14. Honey..our new neighbor's daughter is sunbathing again, come
> > see!
> > 15. I know it's a lot tighter back there but would you please try
> > again?
> > 16. No, No, I'll take the car to have the oil changed.
> > 17. Your mother is way better than mine.
> > 18. Do me a favor, forget the stupid Valentine's day thing and buy
> >   yourself new clubs.
> > 19. I understand fully...our anniversary comes every year for
> > christ's
> >   sake, you go hunting with the guys, it's a wonderful stress
> > reliever.
> > 20. Oh come on, what do ya say we get a good porno movie, a rack of
> >   beer, a few joints, and have my friend Tammy over for a
> > threesome!
> > 21. Christ, not the fucking mall again, come on let's go to that new
> > strip   joint!
> > 22. Listen, I make enough money for the both of us, why don't you
> > retire   and get that nagging handicap down to 7 or 8.
> > 23. You need your sleep ya big silly, now stop getting up for the
> > night   feedings.
> > 24. God if I don't get to blow you soon, I swear I'm gonna bust!
> > 25. I signed up for aerobics so that I can get my ankles behind my
> >   ears for ya...

56. How Dogs and Men Are the Same

While lists of ten may have been traditional for some time, it is clearly late-night talk-show host David Letterman who has featured this format. For examples of the Letterman lists, see *The "Late Night with David Letterman" Book of Top Ten Lists* (New York: Pocket Books, 1990); *An Altogether New Book of Top Ten Lists* (Pocket Books, 1991); *David Letterman's Book of Top Ten Lists* (New York: Bantam Books, 1995); and *David Letterman's New Book of Top Ten Lists* (Bantam Books, 1996).

The first text, collected in Concord, California, via e-mail in December 1996 contains many more than ten comparisons. It consists of an initial listing followed by a reply. The second text bearing the title "Top 10 Reasons Why Dogs Are Better Than Men," a title that by using the phrase "Top 10" would seem to echo the Letterman formula, was collected from Butte, Montana in April 1994. (This text, however, is not contained in the above mentioned Letterman books.) These first two texts, which are decidedly anti-male, are followed by texts three, four, and five, which are equally anti-female. Text three, titled "Why Dogs Are Better Than Women," was collected in June 1997 in Iselin, New Jersey, while texts four and five were collected in Berkeley in May 1994. (For other photocopier comparisons involving fishing or golf as a sexual metaphor, see SD 188–93; WH 214–16.)

How Dogs and Men Are the Same

- ** Both take up too much space on the bed.
- ** Both have irrational fears about vacuum cleaning.
- ** Both are threatened by their own kind.
- ** Both mark their territory.
- ** Both are bad at asking you questions.
- ** Neither tells you what's bothering them.
- ** The smaller ones tend to be more nervous.
- ** Both have an inordinate fascination with women's crotches.
- ** Neither does any dishes.
- ** Both fart shamelessly.
- ** Neither of them notice when you get your hair cut.
- ** Both like dominance games.
- ** Both are suspicious of the postman.
- ** Neither knows how to talk on the telephone.
- ** Neither understands what you see in cats.

And then, the reply by a misanthropic lady, especially of men, and obviously a dog-lover.

How Dogs Are Better Than Men

- ** Dogs do not have problems expressing affection in public.
- ** Dogs miss you when you're gone.
- ** Dogs feel guilt when they've done something wrong.
- ** Dogs don't criticize your friends.
- ** Dogs admit when they're jealous.
- ** Dogs are very direct about wanting to go out.
- ** Dogs do not play games with you – except fetch (and they never laugh at how you throw).
- ** Dogs don't feel threatened by your intelligence.
- ** You can train a dog.
- ** Dogs are easy to buy for.
- ** You are never suspicious of your dog's dreams.
- ** You can't catch any diseases from dogs (OK. The *really* worst disease you can get from them is rabies, but there's a vaccine for it, and you get to kill the one that gives it to you.)
- ** Dogs understand what no means.
- ** Dogs understand if some of their friends cannot come inside.
- ** Middle-aged dogs don't feel the need to abandon you for a younger owner.
- ** Dogs admit it when they're lost.
- ** Dogs are color blind.
- ** Dogs aren't threatened if you earn more than they do.
- ** Dogs mean it when they kiss you.

10. More sophisticated fashion sense
9. Love to dance
8. Willing to sleep on rug and fetch on command
7. Spend less time worrying about hair loss
6. Old buddies don't show up on doorstep unexpectedly
5. Utterly disinterested in professional sports
4. Your parents find them easier to like
3. Rarely jealous of your former boyfriends
2. Willing to hold your purse in public
1. Unlikely to roll over and lose consciousness immediately following intense play

WHY DOGS ARE BETTER THAN WOMEN

Dogs don't cry
Dogs love it when your friends come over.
Dogs don't care if you use their shampoo.
Dogs think you sing great.
A dog's time in the bathroom is confined to a quick drink.
Dogs don't expect you to call when you are running late.
The later you are, the more excited dogs are to see you
Dogs will forgive you for playing with other dogs.
Dogs don't notice if you call them by another dog's name.
Dogs are excited by rough play.
Dogs don't mind if you give their offspring away.
Dogs understand that farts are funny.
Dogs love red meat.
Dogs can appreciate excessive body hair.
Anyone can get a good-looking dog.
If a dog is gorgeous, other dogs don't hate it.
Dogs don't shop.
Dogs like it when you leave lots of things on the floor.
A dog's disposition doesn't change on 28 day cycles.
Dogs never need to examine the relationship.
A dog's parents never visit.
Dogs love long car trips.
Dogs understand that instincts are better then asking for directions.
Dogs understand that all animals smaller than dogs were made to be hunted.
When a dog gets old and starts to snap at you incessantly, you can shoot it.
Dogs like beer.
Dogs don't hate their bodies.
No dog ever bought a Kenny G or Hootie & the Blowfish album.
No dog ever put on 100 pounds after reaching adulthood.
Dogs never criticize.
Dogs agree that you have to raise your voice to get your point across.
Dogs never expect gifts.
It's legal to keep a dog chained up at your house.
Dogs don't worry about germs.
Dogs don't want to know about every other dog you ever had.
Dogs like to do their snooping outside as opposed to in your wallet, desk, and the back of your sock drawer.

Dogs don't let magazine articles guide their lives.
Dogs would rather have you buy them a hamburger dinner than a lobster one.
You never have to wait for a dog. They're ready to go 24 hours a day.
Dogs have no use for flowers, cards, or jewelry.
Dogs don't borrow your shirts.
Dogs never want foot-rubs.
Dogs enjoy heavy petting in public.
Dogs find you amusing when you're drunk.
Dogs can't talk.
Dogs aren't chatty.
Dogs seldom outlive you.

10 Reason Why Fishing Is Better Than Sex

1. A big, juicy worm always gets a fish excited.
2. You don't have to eat a fish while it's still flopping around.
3. You can take a leak in the bush anytime you want.
4. Stroking your rod won't piss off a trout.
5. Sipping a beer and scratching your balls is all the foreplay expected of you.
6. Anything you stick in a fishes face, it eats.
7. A fish will never gag, choke or come up for air.
8. You wear rubbers on your feet, not on your dick.
9. If you want a bigger pole, you can have a bigger pole.
10. It's o.k. to cook a fish to make it taste right.

10 Reason Why A Game Of Golf Is Better Than Sex

1. You get compliments for quick play.
2. Nobody calls you names when you move on to the next hole.
3. Scratching your balls and farting is considered foreplay.
4. No names to remember, all the holes are numbered.
5. Unshaven, fat, old guys can score, same as the young hunks.
6. Everybody gets a shot at the hole, just have to wait your turn.
7. In golf...3 inches, 6 inches, 12 inches are all about the same.
8. Noise in a golf course won't wake the children.
9. A four iron won't get jealous when you stroke your putter.
10. A sub-par performance is something to shout about.

57. What Are the Ten Biggest Lies?

Although in theory "Honesty is always the best policy," and the first president of the United States, George Washington, is revered in part because he is supposed to have said "I cannot tell a lie" (when he confessed he had cut down his father's cherry tree), the fact is that lying is part of the everyday world, from sales to politics, from advertising to attempted sexual seductions. In oral (as opposed to photocopier) tradition there are also lists of lies. For example, there is a 1994 joke: The Three Biggest Lies in Arkansas: 1. The pickup is paid for, 2. I didn't know she was my cousin, and 3. I was just trying to help the pig over the fence.

The following text was collected in Berkeley in September of 1993.

MORE FAX FOLKLORE

What are the ten biggest lies?
1. The check is in the mail.
2. The delivery is on the truck.
3. I promise I won't come in your mouth.
4. It's only a cold sore.
5. I'll still respect you on the morning.
6. I've had a vasectomy.
7. It was owned by a little old lady who only used it to drive her canary to the mountains.
8. It's not the money; it's the principle of the thing.
9. I'm going to leave my wife.
10. This won't hurt a bit.

58. 101 Things Not To Say During Sex

While lying is roundly condemned, there is also the proverb "The truth hurts." Sexual performance can be an activity which causes anxiety. Men and women may worry about being inadequate. The following lengthy item which circulated via e-mail in Moraga, California, in November 1996, provides an extensive list of put-downs of a sexual partner.

101 Things Not to Say During Sex...

1. But everybody looks funny naked!
2. You woke me up for that?
3. Did I mention the video camera?
4. Do you smell something burning?
5. (in a janitor's closet) And they say romance is dead...
6. Try breathing through your nose.
7. A little rug burn never hurt anyone!
8. Is that a Medic-Alert Pendant?
9. Sweetheart, did you lock the back door?
10. But whipped cream makes me break out.
11. Person 1: This is your first time...right?
    Person 2: Yeah...today
12. (in the No Tell Motel) Hurry up! This room rents by the hour!
13. Can you please pass me the remote control?
14. Do you accept Visa?
15. ZZZZZZZZZZZZZZZZZZZZZZZZZZZZZ
16. On second thought, let's turn off the lights.
17. And to think—I was really trying to pick up your friend!
18. So much for mouth-to-mouth.
19. (using body paint) Try not to leave any stains, okay?
20. Hope you're as good looking when I'm sober...
21. (holding a banana) It's just a little trick I learned at the zoo!
22. Do you get any premium movie channels?
23. Try not to smear my make-up, will ya.
24. (preparing to use peanut butter sexually) But I just steam-cleaned this couch!
25. Got any penicillin?
26. But I just brushed my teeth...
27. Smile, you're on Candid Camera!
28. I thought you had the keys to the handcuffs!

29. I want a baby!
30. So much for the fulfillment of sexual fantasies!
31. (in a menage a trois) Why am I doing all the work?
32. Maybe we should call Dr. Ruth . . .
33. Did you know the ceiling needs painting?
34. I think you have it on backwards.
35. When is this supposed to feel good?
36. Put that blender back in the kitchen where it belongs!
37. You're good enough to do this for a living!
38. Is that blood on the headboard?
39. Did I remember to take my pill?
40. Are you sure I don't know you from somewhere?
41. I wish we got the Playboy channel . . .
42. That leak better be from the waterbed!
43. I told you it wouldn't work without batteries!
44. But my cat always sleeps on that pillow.
45. Did I tell you my Aunt Martha died in this bed?
46. If you quit smoking you might have more endurance.
47. No, really . . . I do this part better myself!
48. It's nice being in bed with a woman I don't have to inflate!
49. This would be more fun with a few more people.
50. You're almost as good as my ex!
51. Do you know the definition of statutory rape?
52. Is that you I smell or is it your mattress stuffed with rotten potatoes?
53. You look younger than you feel.
54. Perhaps you're just out of practice.
55. You sweat more than a galloping stallion!
56. They're not cracker crumbs, it's just a rash.
57. Now I know why he/she dumped you . . .
58. Does your husband own a sawed-off shotgun?
59. You give me reason to conclude that foreplay is overrated.
60. What tampon?
61. Have you ever considered liposuction?
62. And to think, I didn't even have to buy you dinner!
63. What are you planning to make for breakfast?
64. I have a confession . . .
65. I was so horny tonight I would have taken a duck home!
66. Are those real or am I just behind the times?
67. Were you by any chance repressed as a child?
68. Is that a hanging sculpture?
69. You'll still vote for me, won't you?
70. Did I mention my transsexual operation?

71. I really hate women who actually think sex means something!
72. Did you come yet, dear?
73. I'll tell you who I'm fantasizing about if you tell me who you're fantasizing about...
74. A good plastic surgeon can take care of that in no time!
75. Does this count as a date?
76. Oprah Winfrey had a show about men like you!
77. Hic! I need another beer for this please.
78. I think biting is romantic—don't you.
79. Q: You can cook, too right?
    A: (Whaddaya think I'm doin'?)
80. When would you like to meet my parents?
81. Man: Maybe it would help if I thought about someone I really like...
    Woman: Yourself?
82. Have you seen "Fatal Attraction"?
83. Sorry about the name tags, I'm not very good with names.
84. Don't mind me. I always file my nails in bed.
85. (in a phone booth) Do you mind if I make a few phone calls?
86. I hope I didn't forget to turn the gas oven off. Do you have a light?
87. Don't worry, my dog's really friendly for a Doberman.
88. Sorry but I don't do toes!
89. You could at least ACT like you're enjoying it!
90. Petroleum jelly or no petroleum jelly, I said NO!
91. Keep it down, my mother is a light sleeper...
92. I'll bet you didn't know I work for "The Enquirer."
93. So that's why they call you MR. Flash!
94. My old girlfriend used to do it a LOT longer!
95. Is this a sin too?
96. I've slept with more women than Wilt Chamberlain!
97. Hey, when is it going to be my friend's turn?
98. Long kisses clog my sinuses...
99. Please understand that I'm only doing this for a raise...
100. How long do you plan to be "almost there"?
101. You mean you're NOT my blind date?

59. Handling Skepticism in Large Crowds

The art of the put-down is by no means confined to the sexual sphere. There are many occasions when a put-down is required to maintain order or to retain self-respect. Hecklers constitute an irritating challenge to performers, including comedians in nightclubs or politicians at the podium. The following item, collected in Walnut Creek, California, in March 1995, offers a practical solution to the problem. For further discussion of the choice term utilized, see SD 64–66.

HANDLING SKEPTICISM IN LARGE CROWDS

"Hey, you...no, not you,

the guy next to you...nope, farther over...

not him...you...no, not you...the guy with

the maroon tie...yes, you! Fuck you!"

60. His Driveway Doesn't Go All the Way Out to the Street

Put-downs may consist of a single word, but they may also be more elaborate. A common insult involves demeaning someone's intelligence. The first of the following texts was collected in Montgomery, Alabama, in September 1991, and it contains a fair sampling of such clichés. A second collected in Petaluma, California, in September 1997, and a third collected in Brooks, California in April 1999 present additional illustrations. There are, however, others in oral tradition, such as "He's a few bricks short of a load" and "He's not the brightest crayon in the box." For a version titled "Playing With Half a Deck," which includes such alternatives as "Two eggs short of an omelette," and "The lights are on, but there's no one at home" and "His upstairs is not fully furnished," see FOJ2, 324. For a version titled "35 Politically Correct Ways to Say Someone's Stupid" taken from the Internet, see *Uncle John's Ultimate Bathroom Reader* (Ashland, Oregon: Bathroom Reader's Press, 1996), 187. See also Jan Harold Brunvand, *The Study of American Folklore*, 4th ed. (New York: W. W. Norton, 1998), p. 96.

HIS DRIVEWAY DOESN'T GO ALL THE WAY OUT TO THE STREET AND OTHER OBSERVATIONS ON THE HUMAN CONDITION

He's 12 shy of a dozen.

She's about as sharp as a bowl of jello.

Her attic's a little dusty.

His car's only got three wheels, and one's going flat.

He doesn't have all the dots on his dice.

He's got the mental agility of a soap dish.

He has both oars in the water, but on the same side of the boat.

He's a couple volts below threshold.

He's got a mind like a steel trap—anything entering gets crushed and mangled.

He's working with an unformatted disk.

There's no wind in the windmills of her mind.

If his IQ was 2 points higher he would be a rock.

In the shopping mall of the mind—he's in the toy department.

Lugnuts rattling in the hubcaps.

Nice house—not much furniture.

Over the Rainbow.

Sailboat fuel for brains.

Surfing in Nebraska.

The gates are down, the lights are flashing, but the train isn't coming.

The synapses are about that far apart.

Too much yardage between the goalposts.

When he plays poker, it's hard to tell whether he has an ace up his sleeve, or if the ace is missing from his deck.

If a thought crossed his mind it would have a long lonely journey.

> 38 Politically correct ways to say someone is stupid
>
>
> 1. A few clowns short of a circus.
>
> 2. A few fries short of a Happy Meal.
>
> 3. An experiment in Artificial Stupidity.
>
> 4. A few beers short of a six-pack.
>
> 5. Dumber than a box of hair.
>
> 6. A few peas short of a casserole.
>
> 7. Doesn't have all her Corn Flakes in one box.
>
> 8. The wheel's spinning, but the hamster's dead.
>
> 9. One Fruit Loop shy of a full bowl.
>
> 10. One taco short of a combination platter.
>
> 11. A few feathers short of a whole duck.
>
> 12. All foam, no beer.
>
> 13. The cheese slid off her cracker.
>
> 14. Body by Fisher, brains by Mattel.
>
> 15. Has an IQ of 2, but it takes 3 to grunt.
>
> 16. Warning: Objects in mirror are dumber than they appear.
>
> 17. Couldn't pour water out of a boot with instructions on the heel.
>
> 18. He fell out of the Stupid tree and hit every branch on the way down.
>
> 19. An intellect rivaled only by garden tools.
>
> 20. As smart as bait.
>
> 21. Chimney's clogged.
>
> 22. Doesn't have all his dogs on one leash.
>
> 23. Doesn't know much, but leads the league in nostril hair.
>
> 24. Elevator doesn't go all the way to the top floor.
>
> 25. Forgot to pay her brain bill.
>
> 26. Her sewing machine's out of thread.
>
> 27. His antenna doesn't pick up all the channels.
>
> 28. His belt doesn't go through all the loops.
>
> 29. If she had another brain, it would be lonely.
>
> 30. Missing a few buttons on his remote control.
>
> 31. No grain in the silo.

```
>
>32. Proof that evolution CAN go in reverse.
>
>33. Receiver is off the hook.
>
>34. Several nuts short of a full pouch.
>
>35. Skylight leaks a little.
>
>36. Slinky's kinked.
>
>37. Surfing in Nebraska.
>
>38. Too much yardage between the goal posts.
>
>
```

These are actual lines from military performance appraisals or OERs (Officer Efficiency Reports)

1. Not the sharpest knife in the drawer,
2. Got into the gene pool while the lifeguard wasn't watching.
3. A room temperature IQ.
4. Got a full 6-pack, but lacks the plastic thingy to hold it all together.
5. A gross ignoramus — 144 times worse than an ordinary ignoramus.
6. A photographic memory but with the lens cover glued on.
7. A prime candidate for natural deselection.
8. Bright as Alaska in December.
9. One-celled organisms out score him in IQ tests.
10. Donated his body to science before he was done using it.
11. Fell out of the family tree.
12. Gates are down, the lights are flashing, but the train isn't coming.
13. Has two brains; one is lost and the other is out looking for it.
14. He's so dense, light bends around him.
15. If brains were taxed, he'd get a rebate.
16. If he were any more stupid, he'd have to be watered twice a week.
17. If you give him a penny for his thoughts, you'd get change.
18. If you stand close enough to him, you can hear the ocean.
19. It's hard to believe that he beat out 1,000,000 other sperm.
20. One neuron short of a synapse.
21. Some drink from the fountain of knowledge; he only gargled.
22. Takes him 1-½ hours to watch 60 minutes.
23. Wheel is turning, but the hamster is dead.

61. Euphemisms for "Self-Gratification"

The larger the number of euphemisms or circumlocutions, the likelier it is that the referent is taboo in any given culture. There is considerable folklore involving masturbation (see SD 194–96), and the folklore includes a number of graphic idioms. The following text was collected in Los Altos, California in 1994. (For a variant of "Polish the weasel," see NT, 53.)

Euphemisms For "Self Gratification"

Spank the monkey
Play with your pocket pal
Loping the mule
Polish the weasel
Launch the pocket rocket
Pull your pudd
Under the cover hitchhiking
Slicing the salami
Yank your chain
Crank your engine
Choke your chicken
Beat your meat

62. The Elementary School

Euphemisms are commonly introduced very early in one's life. Families may employ private code words for basic bodily functions, ranging from "Number 1" and "Number 2" for urination and defecation, to such babytalk terms as "wee wee" or "pee pee" and "ka-ka" or "poo poo." At some point in life, an individual may come to realize that the baby term is not appropriate in the grown-up world. For a list of such terms, see Judith S. Neaman and Carole G. Silver, *A Dictionary of Euphemisms* (London: Unwin, 1983), 53.

The following text was collected in San Francisco in June 1996, and it is based on one of the most common childhood euphemisms. It also refers to one of the modern classics of children's literature. *Winnie-the-Pooh*, by A. A. Milne, first published in October 1926, became an instant favorite. It has also inspired many animated cartoons and motion pictures. The name has been a subject of some curiosity. Apparently the "Winnie" portion came from an American Black Bear by that name who was a popular animal in the London Zoo. "Winnie" supposedly derived from Winnipeg, the home town of the soldier who originally purchased the bear as a cub in White River, Ontario, Canada, according to one source. See Ann Thwaite, *A. A. Milne: The Man Behind Winnie-the-Pooh* (New York: Random House, 1990), 283, 525. However, the "pooh" element remains obscure. One apocryphal account claims that a little girl, a childhood friend of Milne's son, upon smelling the bear at the zoo exclaimed "Oh, Pooh" whereupon Milne's son repeated the phrase (see Thwaite, 284). Hence the association of "pooh" with a bear named "Winnie." To "pooh-pooh" something is to disdain or belittle it, but pooh (and poop) do refer to feces and defecation (cf. a poop deck, a deck at the stern or aft part of a ship, or a pooper-scooper, a small shovel carried by dog owners to pick up their pets' feces from the public street). (For a photocopier folkloristic account of "The Poopie List," see SD 140–41). The apocryphal story cited above does refer to smell and would seem to confirm the fecal association of the phrase that goes back at least to the seventeenth century. Thus to "pooh-pooh" something, meaning to express contempt or disgust, may well be an adult echo of a childhood euphemism.

One day in an elementary school class, the teacher asked the children to stand up and tell their classmates what they'd received for Christmas that year.

The first little girl stood and said "I got a Bow-Wow from my Daddy." The teacher addressed the class and sternly told them that they were certainly old enough to know and use the correct names for things, and that she didn't want to hear any more baby talk. She then asked the little girl if she could think of another word for her gift, one that grown-ups would use.

The little girl replied, "I got a puppy-dog from my Daddy."
The teacher praised her lavishly and went on to the next child, a boy.

"I got a choo-choo for Christmas," he beamed.
Again the teacher chided the little tyke, and asked him to think of another name to describe his gift.

"I got an electric train for Christmas!" he said after mulling it over. The teacher praised him for his efforts.

The next little boy, a normally very quiet kid, stood and said "I got a book," and sat down.

Seeing an opportunity to draw him out a little, the teacher asked "And what was the title of your book?"

The little guy hesitated, and then, with a serious face and a knitted brow, began obvious mental efforts. After a couple of minutes of deep thinking his face brightened and he replied, "Winnie The Shit."

Confirmation of this theme is found in the following brief text reported from Greensburg, Pennsylvania, in May 1997:

> Disney joke:
> Why was Tigger looking in the toilet?
> He was looking for Pooh!

63. Dyslexics Repent!

Dyslexia is a technical term refering to various reading disabilities, one of the most characteristic of which involves word and letter reversal. Thus the word "saw" is mistakenly read as "was," or the letter "d" may be misread as "p" or "b." While it presents a fairly serious problem for those who suffer from the affliction, it, like other disabilities (e.g., stuttering, blindness, quadriplegia, cleft palate, etc.), does provide a topic for traditional folk humor. Typical oral jokes on the subject include: "Did you hear about the bumper sticker: 'Dyslexics of the World Untie' "? or "Did you hear about the dyslexic rabbi who said 'Yo!' "? and "Did you hear about the dyslexic who tried to commit suicide by jumping behind a bus"?

Dyslexia is also featured in photocopier folklore. The following item was collected in Montgomery, Alabama, in 1990. A second, unrelated item was collected in Walnut Creek, California in 1988. It is a parody of the acronym for the organization known as Mothers Against Drunk Driving [MADD]. A third text, collected in Storrs, Connecticut, in February 1997, is also found in oral tradition.

DYSLEXICS
REPENT!
EJUSS
DIED FOR YOUR
SNIS!

> In Arizona I met a group who's cause I think we should seriously consider supporting
>
> ## D. A. M.
>
> <u>M</u>others <u>A</u>gainst <u>D</u>islexgia
>
> Boy do they need help

Did you hear about the agnostic, dyslectic insomniac? He stayed up all night, wondering whether there was really a Dog.

64. Learning to Spell with "Darnell"

Making fun of dyslexia does not involve any ethnic connotation. However, ethnic speech patterns and regional dialects are frequent subjects of traditional humor. Within any ethnic or regional group, there may be a tension between speaking in dialect and speaking the mainstream language. Some parents want their children to speak the latter properly (for purposes of social mobility and economic advantage); others fear that speaking the mainstream language constitutes a form of assimilation, which denigrates and diminishes their original speech pattern.

Nowhere is this issue more clearly delineated than in the concerted effort on the part of educators to encourage African American children to speak so-called standard English. The issue received national prominence in early 1997 when the Oakland, California School Board announced plans to "recognize" Black speech as a separate language that was termed "Ebonics." It did not take long for the folk to update an item already in tradition to comment on this particular linguistic proposal.

The first version was collected in Walnut Creek, California in 1992. The second version, originally titled "Leroy's Homework," was given a new label following the Oakland School Board proclamation: "Hooked on Ebonics." For another version of this item, see FOJ2, 448–49. (For other examples of dialect humor in photocopier tradition, see WH, 23–24, 129–31; WY, 39–41, 253–54; NT 33–35; SD, 76, 81–92; 107–08, 124–25.

This is Learning to Spell with Darnell. I be Darnell Jackson, and today we're gonna spell the word _____ . Spell it with me now, _ _ _ _ _ _ _ _ _ _ . Now let's use it in a sentence . . .

Foreclose	"If I don't pay any alimony this month, I'll have more money forclose."
Sodomy	"When I go out at night I like one bitch on one sodomy and another bitch on the other sodomy."
Rectum	"I had two Cadillacs, but my girlfriend rectum both.
Hotel	"I gave my girlfriend the crabs then hotel everybody."
Decide	"My favorite girls are Wanda and Yolanda, but I like to keep a couple on decide."

Disappointment	"My parole officer told me, If I miss disappointment, he's going to send me back to the big house."
Penis	I saw my parole officer the other day and he handed me a little paper cup and said, here penis."
Afford	"I wanted to buy a Cadillac, but then I had to settle for afford."
Subpoena	"I went to the 2 Live Crew concert the other night and the lines were so long at the johns, subpoena the sink."
Manual	"I told my buddy Tyrone, manual get yourself in trouble if you keep messing with that hoe."
Catacomb	"I went to the Douglas/Holyfield fight last week and sat next to Don King, now someone oughta get that catacomb."
Mister	"My girlfriend went on vacation and I really mister."
Undermine	"There's a fine looking bitch living in the apartment undermine."
Cadaver	"I told my buddy Tyrone that I liked his sister and wanted to see her, and he said I cadaver."
Paramour	"I was playing cards with my buddy _____ and I said what you got? He said I got an Ace high and you're going to need a paramour to beat me."
Polyp	"On my way home from the Piston's game the other night, I was involved in a five car polyp on I-75."
Urinal	"After the police broke down my front door last night, they said, Darnell Jackson urinal lot of trouble!"
Israel	"Some guy tried to sell me a Rolex watch the other day, I said hey man that looks fake! He said no man that watch Israel!"
Assert	"On the way home from work, I always take assert so my old lady don't smell liquor on my breath."
Cantilever	"My old lady just bitch, bitch, bitch, but no matter how hard I try, I just cantilever."

Wordplay

Acoustic — "On my ninth birthday my Uncle Rufus bought me acoustic and then took me to the pool hall."

Condom — "The man I sold a watch to says it was no good and I should take it back. He said I condom."

Beware — "I asked the man at the employment office, is this beware I find me a job?"

Stain — "My sister and brother-in-law stopped by the other day, so I asked them, you plan on stain?"

Derange — "Derange is where the deer and the antelope play."

Income — "My girlfriend and I just got into bed when income my wife."

Iraq — "My buddy Jarvis and I went down to the pool hall on Saturday. I said Iraq and you break."

Seldom — "I had two extra tickets to the basketball game the other night, so I seldom to my friend."

Letter — "The ugly bitch downstairs came knocking on Darnell's door the other night, but I wouldn't letter in."

Vitamin — "When the preacher man come knocking on my door to see my mama, I always vitamin."

Semen — "I never did know who my papa was cause my mama semen left and right."

Data — "At my basketball game the other night, I scored a triple double, and my coach said data boy Darnell.

Honor — "At our rape trial the judge asked my buddy Jarvis, who be honor first?"

Clothesline — "When I came home late again, I found my clothesline on the porch."

Odyssey — "When I got back from the Windsor Ballet, I told my friends, you odyssey the (bleep) on that babe!"

Mannequin — "I saw Michael Jordan at the Palace the other night. The mannequin sure play some ball!"

Horde	"My mamma always did have a bad reputation because she horde around in high school.
Homo	The bitch I'm living with called me at the bar the other night. She said, Darnell honey, are you coming homo what?"
Tripoli	I tried to buy my girlfriend Dorita some underwear the other day but couldn't find any, she take size 38 Tripoli.
Candidate	"I saw my buddy Melvin the other day. I said Melvin, candidate your mama?"
Fortify	"I asked this bitch down on 6 Mile—How Much? She said fortify dollars honey."
Baghdad	"I always wondered what was in the Baghdad use to drink out of when he was sitting on the front porch."
Dimension	"A lot of you ladies been calling in wondering what Darnell look like. Well I'm tall, dark, handsome, not dimension hung like a horse."
Photo	"I went down to the chop shop to buy me a car. The man asked me, do you want a two-door or photo?"
Button	"My girlfriend Juanita bought some leopard skin stretch pants. I said girl you won't get your button them!"
July	"After the trial, my mama asked me, did you tell the truth or July?"
Potato	"All my friends are always trying to tell me what's going down, potato know shit!"
Fascinate	"My sister Wolanda bought a sweater with ten buttons on it, but her tits are so big she can only fascinate!"
Ididarod	"When my car quit working, I went to see Mr. Goodwrench. He said, Ididarod."
Widen	"When my girlfriend Latrine told me she was pregnant I said, widen you tell me you didn't use no birth control?"

Adobe	"After my apartment was broken into, the policeman asked me, how'd they get in? I said adobe open out back."
Oreo	"I told my friend Alonzo, if he wanted my sister, he could pay me $50 bucks now oreo me $100 bucks on Friday."
Harassment	"I talked to Judge Thomas the other day and he said about that Anita Hill, he never wodda gotten involved if he knew what harassment."

HOOKED ON EBONICS

Leroy is an 18year old 10th grader. This is Leroy's homework assignment in which he was instructed to use each vocabulary word in a sentence.

1. Foreclose: If I pay alimony this month, I got no money foreclose.
2. Rectum: I had two cadillacs, but my ol' lady rectum both.
3. Hotel: I gave my girlfriend crabs and the hotel everybody.
4. Disappointment: My parole officer tol' me if I miss disappointment they gonna send me to da big house.
5. Penis: I went to da doctor and he handed me a cup and said penis.
6. Israel: Alonso tried to sell me a Rolex. I said, man that looks fake. He said bullshit, that watch Israel.
7. Catacomb: Don King was at da fight the other night, man somebody oughta give dat catacomb.
8. Undermine: There is a fine lookin hoe living in the apartment undermine.
9. Acoustic: When I was little, my uncle bought me acoustic and took me to da pool hall.
10. Iraq: When we go to da pool hall, I tol my uncle Iraq, you break.
11. Stain: My mother-in-law stopped by and I axed her, do you plan on stain for dinner?
12. Seldom: My cousin gave me two tickets to the Nicks game, so I seldom.
13. Honor: At the rape trial, the Judge axed my buddy, who be honor first?
14: Odyssey: I tol my brother, you odyssey the tits on that hoe.
15: Axe: The policeman wanted to axe me some questions.
16: Tripoli: I was gonna buy my old lady a bra for her birthday, but I couldn't find no tripoli.
17: Fortify: I axed the hoe how much? She said fortify.
18: Income: I just got into bed with da hoe and income my wife.

65. Hebonics

Obviously inspired by the Ebonics debate, we have an item that claims to be a Jewish equivalent, namely, "Hebonics." It was collected in Berkeley, California in June 1997. This combination of Yiddish and English is sometimes referred to as "Yinglish," a formation with parallels involving other combinations with English, e.g., Spenglish for Spanish and English. For additional discussions of Yiddish loanwords, inflections, and other speech characteristics, see Leo Rosten, *The Joys of Yiddish* (New York: Pocket Books, 1968); Martin Marcus, *Yiddish For Yankees* (Philadelphia: J. B. Lippincott, 1968), Arthur Naiman, *Every Goy's Guide to Common Jewish Expressions* (New York: Ballatine, 1981), Gene Bluestein, *Anglish-Yinglish: Yiddish in American Life and Literature* (Athens: University of Georgia Press, 1989), Molly Katz, *Jewish as a Second Language* (New York: Workman Publishing, 1991), and Yetta Emmes, *Drek: The Real Yiddish Your Bubbe Never Taught You* (New York, 1998).

The Jewish Grandmother's language: Jewish English or "Hebonics"

The Encino School Board has declared Jewish English a second language.

Backers of the move say the district is the first in the nation to recognize Hebonics as the language of many of America's Jews. Here are some descriptions of the characteristics of the language, and samples of phrases in standard English and Jewish English.

Samples of Pronunciation Characteristics

Jewish English or "Hebonics" hardens consonants at the ends of words. Thus, "hand" becomes "handt."

The letter "W" is always pronounced as if it were a "V". Thus "walking" becomes "valking"

"R" sounds are transformed to a guttural utterance that is virtually impossible to spell in English. It is "ghraining" "algheady"

Samples of Idiomatic Characteristics

Questions are always answered with questions:

Question: "How do you feel?"
Hebonics response: "How should I feel?"

The subject is often placed at the end of a sentence after a pronoun has been used at the beginning: "She dances beautifully, that girl."

The sarcastic repetition of words by adding "sh" to the front is used for emphasis:
mountains becomes "shmountains"
turtle becomes "shmurtle"

Sample Usage Comparisons

Standard English Phrase: Hebonics Phrase:
"He walks slow"   "Like a fly in the ointment he walks"
"You're sexy"
"Sorry, I do not know the time"   "What do I look like, a clock?"
"I hope things turn out for the best"   "You should BE so lucky"
"Anything can happen"   "It is never so bad, it can't get worse."

66. Rune-Sore-Bees?

One of the largest and fastest growing minority populations in the United States speaks Spanish. Native Spanish-speaking individuals have their own particular problems in learning to speak English. Some of the immigrants, legal and illegal, from Mexico and other Latin American countries are forced to take menial, entry-level jobs, e.g., as maids and food service employees. In the following item reported from San Mateo, California, in 1995, collected from a Chilean-American, "Spanglish" or "Spenglish" is featured. In this parody, it is not the immigrant's problem in understanding "Spenglish." For further examples of this linguistic hybrid, see Ricky Herrera, *How to espeak Spenglish* (Coral Gables, Fl.: Lay Back and Read Books, 1987).

Reading hints: You are on the phone. The other party is also in the hotel.

Morny, rune sore-bees

Oh sorry, I thought I dialed room service.

Rye. Rune sore-bees. Morny. Jewish to odor sunteen?

Yes order something. This is room thirteen-oh-five. I want...

Okay, torino-fie. Yes plea?

I'd like some bacon and eggs.

Ow july then?

What?

Aches. Ow july then? Pry, boy, pooch...?

Oh, the eggs! How do I like them! Sorry. Scrambled, please.

Ow july thee baycome? Crease?

Crisp will be fine.

Okay. An Santos?

What?

Santos. July Santos?

Uh... I don't know... I don't think so.

No? Judo one toes?

Look, I really feel bad about this, but I just don't know what judo-one-toes means. I'm sorry...

Toes! Toes! Why Jew Don Juan toes? Ow bow eenlish mopping we bother?

English muffin! I've got it! Toast! You were saying toast! Fine. An English muffin will be fine.

We bother?

No just put the bother on the side.

Wad?

I'm sorry. I meant butter. Butter on the side.

Copy?

I feel terrible about this but...

Copy. Copy, tea, mil...

Coffee! Yes, coffee please. And that's all.

One Minnie. Ass rune torino-fie, strangle eches, crease baycome, tossy eenlish mopping we bother honey sigh, and copy. Rye?

Whatever you say.

Okay. Tenjewberrymud.

You're welcome.

67. The Little Rascals

Stereotype speech can also be found in old movies. Typically, African American characters spoke in thick, southern Black-dialect while Caucasians displayed perfect English diction. From 1922 to 1944, there was a series of over two hundred films produced by Hal Roach involving a diverse group of children. The names of the characters in *Our Gang* included Alfalfa, Spanky, Darla, and Buckwheat, a Black child. These films were later recycled and renamed "The Little Rascals," to be shown on television in the 1950s, which gave them a new lease on life and introduced them to another generation. The following item was collected in Eurgene, Oregon in December 1996. For a thorough discussion of these films, see Leonard Maltin and Richard W. Bann, *Our Gang: The Life and Times of the Little Rascals* (New York: Crown Publishers, 1977).

The little rascals were in class and the teacher was giving them a vocabulary lesson. The teacher said, "Alfalfa, use the word love in a sentence."

Alfalfa replies, "I love Darla."

The teacher said, "Good . . . now Spanky your word is respect."

Spanky replies, "I respect the way Alfalfa loves Darla."

The teacher said, "Very good! Now Buckweat its your turn, your word is Dictate."

Buckweat replies, "Hey Darla . . . how did my dictate last night?"

68. Questions of Life

There are peculiarities of speech even in mainstream languages. Some of these oddities are classified as "idioms," as if to admit that they do not conform to common grammatical rules or to common sense. The delight in paradox and seeming contradiction is very evident in the following ingenious text collected in Petaluma, California in June 1995. A second version was collected in Eugene, Oregon in December 1996. A third version comes from the San Bernardino State University campus in California, in March 1997. A fourth version circulated in the San Francisco Bay Area in October of 1999. A fifth version also from San Francisco dates from July, 1999. Other titles of the item include "Why Ask Why," and "Just Wondering." Some individual questions are in oral tradition, such as "Do Witches use Spell check?" or the feminist-inspired "If a man speaks in the woods [forest], and no [woman] one hears him, is he still wrong?" Other questions contained in versions not presented here include: "If a mute swears, does his mother wash his hands with soap?" and "When sign makers go on strike, is anything written on their signs?" and "Does distressed leather come from very tense cows?" and "If the #2 pencil is the most popular, why is it still #2?"

QUESTIONS OF LIFE

1. Why do you need a driver's license to buy liquor when you can't drink and drive?
2. Why isn't phonetic spelled the way it sounds?
3. Why are there Interstates in Hawaii?
4. Why are there flotation devices under plane seats instead of parachutes?
5. Why are cigarettes sold at gas stations where smoking is prohibited?
6. Do you need a silencer if you are going to shoot a mime?
7. Have you ever imagined a world without hypothetical situations?
8. How does the guy who drives the snowplow get to work?
9. If 7-11 is open 24 hours a day, 365 days a year, why are there locks on the doors?
10. If a cow laughs, does milk come out its nose?
11. If nothing ever sticks to Teflon, how do they make Teflon stick to the pan?
12. If buttered toast always lands buttered side down on the floor and a cat always lands on its feet, what would happen if you tied a piece of buttered toast to the back of a cat and dropped it?

13. If you are driving at the speed of light and turn on your headlights, what happens?
14. You know how most packages say "open here", what is the prototocol if the package says "open somewhere else"?
15. Why do they put Braille dots on the keypad of the drive up ATM?
16. Why do we drive on parkways and park on driveways?
17. Why is brassiere singular and panties plural?
18. Why is it that when you transport something by car its called shipment, but when you transport something by ship its called cargo?
19. You know that indestructible black box that is used on airplanes, why can't they make the whole plane out of the same substance?
20. Why is it that when you are driving and looking for an address, you turn the radio down?
21. Why don't sheep shrink when it rains?
22. Why are they called apartments when they are all stuck together?
23. What does Geronimo say when he jumps out of a plane?
24. If fire fighters fight fires, and crime fighters fight crime, what do freedom fighters fight?
25. If con is the opposite of pro, is Congress the opposite of progress?
26. If olive oil comes from olives, where does baby oil come from?

Subject: Life's Questions:

Why is there never an answer to the most important questions in life?

Why doesn't glue stick to the inside of the bottle?

Can fat people go skinny-dipping?

Can you be a closet claustrophobic?

Why is the word abbreviation so long?

Is it possible to be totally partial?

What's another word for thesaurus?

If a book about failures doesn't sell, is it a success?

If the funeral procession is at night, do folks drive with their lights off?

When companies ship styrofoam, what do they pack it in?

If you're cross-eyed and have dyslexia, can you read all right?

If a stealth bomber crashes in a forest, will it make a sound?

If the cops arrest a mime, do they tell him he has the right to remain silent?

If a parsley farmer is sued, can they garnish his wages?

When it rains, why don't sheep shrink?

Should vegetarians eat animal crackers?

Do cemetery workers prefer the graveyard shift?

What do you do when you see an endangered animal that eats only endangered plants?

Do hungry crows have ravenous appetites?

More Thoughts to Ponder

If you throw a cat out a car window does it become kitty litter?
If corn oil comes from corn, where does baby oil come from?
If there is no God, who pops up the next Kleenex in the box?
When a cow laughs does milk come up its nose?
Why do they put Braille on the number pads of drive-through bank machines?
How did a fool and his money GET together?
If nothing sticks to Teflon, how do they stick Teflon on the pan?
How do they get a deer to cross at that yellow road sign?
If it's tourist season, why can't we shoot them?
What's another word for thesaurus?
Why do they sterilize the needles for lethal injections?
What do they use to ship Styrofoam?
Why is abbreviation such a long word?
Why is there an expiration date on my sour cream container?
Why do kamikaze pilots wear helmets?
How do you know when it's time to tune your bagpipes?
Is it true that cannibals don't eat clowns because they taste funny?
When you choke a smurf, what color does it turn?
Does fuzzy logic tickle?
Why do they call it a TV set when you only get one?
Do radioactive cats have 18 half-lives?
If you shoot a mime, should you use a silencer?
What was the best thing before sliced bread?
If one synchronized swimmer drowns, do the rest have to drown too?

Imponderables:

> Do cemetery workers prefer the graveyard shift?

> Do Lipton employees take coffee breaks?

> How do a fool and his money GET together?

> How do you know when it's time to tune your bagpipes?

> How is it that a building burns up as it burns down?

> If the pen is mightier than the sword, and a picture is worth a thousand words, how dangerous is a fax?

> What hair color do they put on the driver's licenses of bald men?

> Why do banks charge you a "non-sufficient funds" fee on money they already know you don't have?

> Why do they sterilize the needles for lethal injections?

> If Barbie is so popular, why do you have to buy her friends?

> If one synchronized swimmer drowns, do the rest have to drown too?

> In a country of free speech, why are there phone bills?

> How come there aren't B batteries?

> How do I set my laser printer on stun?

> How is it possible to have a civil war?

> If all the world is a stage, where is the audience sitting?

> If love is blind, why is lingerie so popular?

> Why is the alphabet in that order? Is it because of that song?

> If I melt dry ice, can I take a bath without getting wet?

> Crime doesn't pay ... does that mean that my job is a crime?

> How can there be self-help "groups"?

> How do they get the deer to cross at that yellow road sign?

> How do you know honesty is the best policy until you have tried some of the others?

> How does a Thermos know if the drink should be hot or cold?

> How does the guy who drives the snowplow get to work in the mornings?

> If a word in the dictionary is misspelled, how would we know?

> What happens to an 18-hour bra after 18 hours?

> Why didn't Noah swat those two mosquitoes?

> Why do tourists go to the tops of tall buildings and then put money into telescopes so they can see things on the ground close-up?

> What if the Hokey Pokey IS what it's all about?

Deep Thoughts

> >
> >If people from Poland are called "Poles", why aren't people from Holland called "Holes"?
> >
> >When cheese gets its picture taken, what does it say?
> >
> >Why are a wise man and a wise guy opposites?
> >
> >If horrific means to make horrible, does terrific mean to make terrrible?
> >
> >Why isn't 11 pronounced as onety one?
> >
> >Do infants enjoy infancy as much as adults enjoy adultery?
> >
> >Why is a person who plays the piano called a pianist, but a person who drives a race car not called a racist?
> >
> >Why do women wear evening gowns to nightclubs? Shouldn't they be wearing nightgowns?
> >
> >When someone asks you, "A penny for your thoughts", and you put your two cents in, what happens to the other penny?
> >
> >Why is the man who invests all your money called a broker?
> >
> >If you mixed vodka with orange juice and milk of magnesia, would you get a Phillips Screwdriver?
> >
> >"I am" is reportedly the shortest sentence in the English language. Could it be that "I do" is the longest?
> >
> >Do Roman paramedics refer to IV's as "4's"?
> >
> >If a pig loses its voice, is it disgruntled?
> >
> >If you take an Oriental person and spin him around several times, does he become disoriented?
> >

69. Proof That Horses Have an Infinite Number of Legs

If there are propositions which defy logic, there are examples of logic which lead to absurd propositions. The following silly syllogism is a parody of deductive reasoning involving "four play." It was collected in Chicago in 1994.

PROOF THAT HORSES HAVE AN INFINITE NUMBER OF LEGS

- Horses have an even number of legs.

- They have two legs in back and fore legs in front.

- This makes a total of six legs, which certainly is an odd number of legs for a horse.

- But the only number that is both odd and even is infinity,

- Therefore, horses must have an infinite number of legs

70. The Bumblebee Cannot Fly

In nature as in language, there are seeming paradoxes. For example, there are birds that cannot fly, e.g., ostriches and emus. And there are mammals that can fly, e.g., bats. Among such apparent anomalies is the bumblebee, which appears to be too heavy to fly.

The following item was collected in Northport, New York, in 1996 but with an indication that it dates from the 1940s. This is of interest inasmuch as the story of the bumblebee's theoretically being unable to fly supposedly circulated in German technical universities in the early 1930s. See John H. McMasters, "The Flight of the Bumblebee and Related Myths of Entomological Engineering," *American Scientist* 77 (1989), 164–69. According to one version of the story, a Swiss professor, an expert in aerodynamics, was engaged in dinner conversation with a biologist who questioned him about the aerodynamic principles governing bumblebee flight. After some hasty preliminary calculations, the Swiss authority claimed that he had "proved" the bee to be incapable of flight. He later recanted, indicating that his initial calculations had been in error, but it was too late, and the story had already entered into oral tradition, becoming bona fide folklore. This folklore, however, continues to intrigue scientists. See, for example, Jeremy M. V. Rayner, "The Flight of the Bumblebee," *Nature* 347 (4 December 1990), 422–23. The double entendre at the end of the item may reflect the traditional euphemistic allusion to sexual activity as the province of "the birds and the bees."

THE BUMBLEBEE CANNOT FLY

According to the theory of aerodynamics, and as may be readily demonstrated through experiments, the bumblebee is unable to fly. This is because the size, the weight, and the shape of his body, in relation to his wingspread, make flying impossible.

But the bumblebee, being ignorant of these scientific truths, goes ahead and flies anyway—and makes a little honey every day.

71. The Chicken Gun

Birds in flight can sometimes constitute a serious hazard to air traffic. If one or more birds hit the cockpit or are sucked into a jet engine, a plane may be at risk. The danger is greatest at lower elevations, e.g., when the plane is taking off or landing. The following item is not only a commentary on the Federal Aviation Administration, one of the agencies responsible for air safety, but is also a gibe at the supposed lack of intelligence of the British. It was collected from an electrical engineering major at UCLA in 1996.

The Chicken Gun

In a recent issue of "Meat & Poultry" magazine, editors quoted from "Feathers," the publication of the California Poultry Industry Federation, telling the following story:

It seems the US Federal Aviation Administration has a unique device for testing the strength of windshields on airplanes. The device is a gun that launches a dead chicken at a plane's windshield at approximately the speed the plane flies.

The theory is that if the windshield doesn't crack from the carcass impact, it'll survive a real collision with a bird during flight. It seems the British were very interested in this and wanted to test

windshield on a brand new, speedy locomotive they're developing.

They borrowed the FAA's chicken launcher, loaded the chicken and fired. The ballistic chicken shattered the windshield, went through the engineer's chair, broke an instrument panel and embedded itself

the back wall of the engine cab. The British were stunned and asked the FAA to recheck the test to see if everything was done correctly.

The FAA reviewed the test thoroughly and had one recommendation:

"Use a thawed chicken."

72. ValuJet Advertising Slogans

Despite the best efforts of airlines and the federal regulatory agencies, tragic air crashes do occur. On May 11, 1996, a ValuJet DC-9 plummeted into the Florida Everglades killing all the 110 people aboard. As so often happens after a nationally publicized disaster, sick humor began to surface. In less than a month following the sad event, a set of purported ValueJet slogans made their appearance. Even though, statistically speaking, the chances of an air crash are far, far less than the occurrence of a fatal automobile accident, the media invariably focuses on each and every air disaster. One reason for this emphasis is the general public's malaise with respect to air travel. In an airplane, the individual passenger has no control over the fate of the plane and is totally dependent upon the pilot's skill and the mechanical state of the aircraft. Additionally, there is the fear of falling and the recognition that in a case of impending death, whether caused by malfunction, pilot error, or by terrorist intervention, there may be moments of panic before the end comes. In any event, sick or not, the public response to air tragedies includes a kind of humor.

The first text was collected in Berkeley in 1988 following several crashes involving Delta Airlines. It is clearly the direct model for the second text, which is representative of the ValuJet photocopier tradition. This demonstrates that photocopier folklore, like all folklore, can be recycled whenever deemed appropriate to fit new contexts. It was collected in Alton, Illinois on June 24, 1996. A third item, also a folk commentary on the status of one aspect of air travel, was collected by a United Airlines pilot from a bulletin board at the United Airlines terminal in Denver, Colorado in December 1995.

FIFTEEN REASONS TO FLY DELTA

1. DELTA: We never make the same mistake three times!
2. DELTA: A REAL MAN LANDS WHERE HE WANTS TO.
3. DELTA: Terrorists are afraid to fly with us!
4. DELTA: We're AMTRAK with wings.
5. DELTA: Join our Frequent Near-miss Program!
6. DELTA: Noisy engines? We'll turn 'em off!
7. DELTA: Ask about our out-of-court settlements.
8. DELTA: Enjoy the in-flight movie on the plane next to you.
9. DELTA: The kids will LOVE our inflatable slides.
10. DELTA: Bring a bathing suit!
11. DELTA: Enjoy complimentary champagne during free-fall.
12. DELTA: Our pilots are terminally ill and have nothing to lose.
13. DELTA: We might be landing on YOUR street!
14. DELTA: If you think it's so easy, get your own @#%!@#$ plane!
15. DELTA: DELTA gets you CLOSE.

Top 22 "ValuJet" advertising slogans

1. ValuJet: When you just can't wait for the world to come to you.

2. ValuJet: We're Amtrak with wings.

3. Join our frequent near-miss program.

4. On certain flights, every section is a smoking section.

5. Ask about our out-of-court settlements.

6. Our staff has had lots of experience consoling next-of-kin.

7. Are our jets too noisy? Don't worry. We'll turn them off.

8. Complimentary champagne during free-fall.

9. Enjoy the in-flight movie in the plane next to you.

10. ValuJet: The Kids Will Love Our Inflatable Slides.

11. Valujet: You Think It's So Easy, Get Your Own Damn Plane!

12. Which will fall faster, our stock price or our planes?

13. Our pilots are all terminally ill and have nothing to lose.

14. ValuJet: We may be landing in your backyard.

15. ValuJet: Terrorists are afraid to fly with us.

16. ValuJet: Bring a bathing suit.

17. Some airlines are content to fly thousands of feet over landmarks. We try to get as close as possible for the best view.

18. That guy who crashed into the White House was one of our best pilots.

19. Fly ValuJet: Find out if there really is a God.

20. ValuJet: A real man lands where he wants to.

21. ValuJet: So That's What Those Buttons Do!

22. ValuJet: We Never Make the Same Mistake Three Times.

73. Dear Captayn

Even little children may manifest concern about the safety of their flight. Perhaps the fear of flying is wittingly or unwittingly communicated to a child by an anxious parent. Children are also relatively familiar with air travel thanks to television and motion pictures. The following item collected in Iselin, New Jersey, in 1993, plays upon the presumed innocence of young children, an innocence conveyed both by the writing style and by the accompanying drawings.

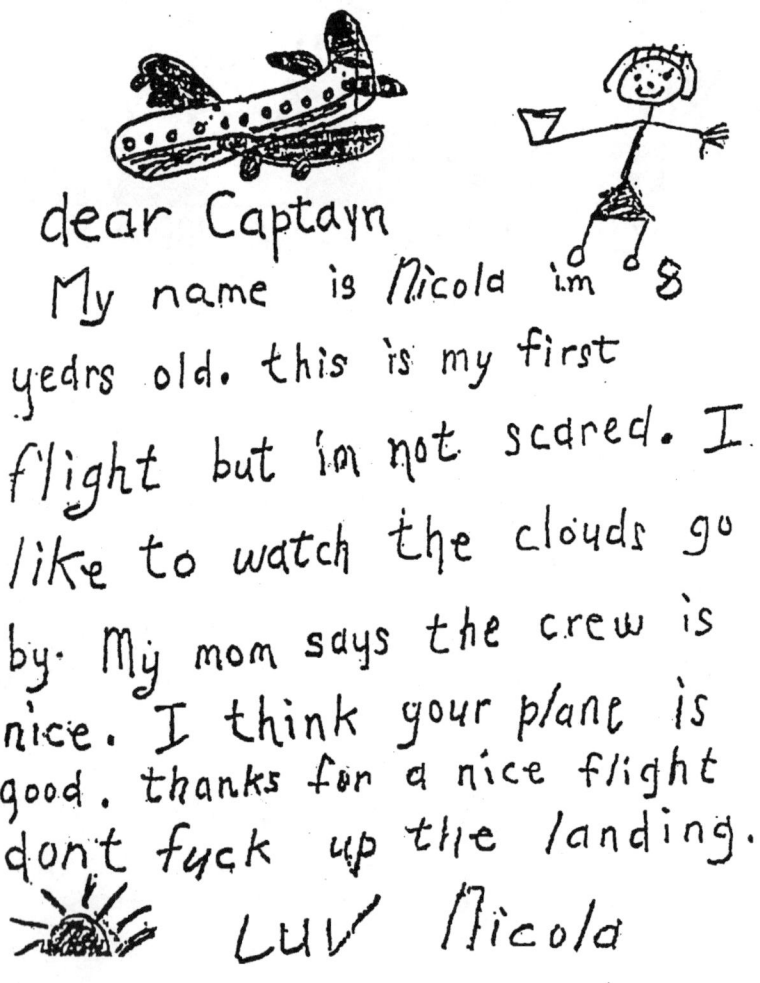

dear Captayn
My name is Nicola i'm 8 yedrs old. this is my first flight but im not scared. I like to watch the clouds go by. My mom says the crew is nice. I think your plane is good. thanks for a nice flight dont fyck up the landing.
LuV Nicola

74. What the Captain Means Is...

The folklore of air travel extends beyond commercial aviation to include military flight. The pressures of serving on active duty are such that a rich tradition has flourished to provide an outlet for the articulation of inevitable anxieties. Traditions run the gamut from cadence counts in boot camp to bawdy folksongs and off-color jokes. Fearful of the public's possible reaction to uncensored military personnel opinion, the government provides professional public relations experts to translate such opinion into acceptable prose. The following two versions of a classic piece of military folklore illustrate the difference between the supposed real jargon of an Air Force captain and the sanitized version offered to the media.

The first version was collected in Oakland, California, in 1980, but it clearly refers to the Korean War of 1950–52 and undoubtedly dates from the 1950s. The second version is set in Vietnam and was collected in 1968. It was first published by Joseph F. Tuso, a Major in the United States Air Force who served on the faculty of the Department of English at the United States Air Force Academy. See "A Folk Drama—'What the Captain Means Is...' or That Interview You Never Saw on TV," *Folklore Forum*, 5 (1) (January 1972), 25–27. Except for occasional phrases in common such as "I don't care which way the runway runs," the two versions are quite different textually. However, the technique is basically the same, that is, a series of blunt uncouth statements followed by a series of censored translations. For other examples of this technique in photocopier tradition, see WH 51–56.

For a very brief discussion of a version which Legman reports circulated during World War II, see NLM, 332. Even though he does not present a full text of this item, which he calls a "hilarious 'send-up,'" the discussion does document the fact that this piece of folklore has served in at least three different wars. For other examples of this technique in photocopier tradition, see WH 51–56; WY, 29–33; NT, 30–31; and SD, 70–71.

(An interview between Capt. Claghorn, Jr., America's leading war ace just returned from Korea, the Press, and Major Wilsan of Pentagon Relations)

Press: Welcome home Capt., how do you feel being back in the States again?

Capt.: Pretty pissed off.

Major: (to the press) Capt. Claghorn's eyes were misty when the outline of the Statue of Liberty, symbol of American faith for liberty, loomed into sight.

Press: What is the first thing you are going to do in New York, Capt.?

Capt: Get laid.

Major: He intends to fly back to his old home town immediately and see his mom and all his folks.

Press: Are they going to give you the Congressional Medal of Honor?

Capt.: They damn well should.

Major: Junior's modesty disclaims all high awards. "Every man in the battle line deserves it as much as I," the Ace said.

Press: What about the case of champagne Col. Hess was going to give you for breaking Campbell's record?

Capt.: He crapped out on me.

Major: Capt. Claghorn is a teetootaller, the price of a case was generously donated to Cheju-do at his suggestion.

Press: How did you shoot down all those planes?

Capt.: I guess I'm a pretty fucking hot pilot.

Major: Bashful Junior attributes all his success to a combination of teamwork, luck and superior equipment.

Press: Do you think the Chinese pilot is as good as the American?

Capt.: I can fly circles up their asses.

Major: He pays high tribute to the fighting skill of the enemy.

Press: What about the Russians?

Capt.: Those shitheads. They don't know their asses from third base.

Major: What the Capt. means is the quality of the Russian Airmen is declining.

Press: What about your mechanic? Was he pretty good?

Capt.: That dumb son of a bitch was born with his thumb up his ass. It was a miracle I ever got off the ground.

Major:	The Capt. is lavish of his praise for our courageous ground crews who work day and night to keep them flying.
Press:	We understand that you aim to visit the factory that made your plane.
Capt.:	Yes, if the bastards aren't on strike, I'd like to get my hands on the asshole that welded his lunch box into the tail section of my ship.
Major:	He is proud of our American workers and the magnificent job they are doing "Backing the attack."
Press:	What is your opinion of the Korean women?
Capt.:	I don't give a crap whether the runway runs N-S or E-W. A shack job's a shack job.
Major:	Junior states that he never noticed them as he was always dreaming of his childhood sweetheart.
Press:	What influenced you to join the gallant Airforce?
Capt.:	Shit, I thought I was joining a peacetime outfit, then the bastards shafted me just when I was functioning with the women.
Major:	The Capt. says "When there is a fight, I want to be in the fightingest outfit."
Press:	I understand that you intend to teach gunnery before going back.
Capt.:	Yea, somebody's got to give these kids the ungarbled word. The stuff they taught me in training almost caused me to get my ass shot off.
Major:	Capt. Claghorn is unqualified in his praise of the high degree of training given our fledgling pilots.
Press:	Ah' (he is interrupted by Capt.)
Capt.:	Sorry boys, I've got to get out of here before the bars close and line up a piece of ass, so long.
Major:	Yes, Capt. Claghorn can't wait to get back to his mother's pies and the girl he left behind.

The following exchange occurs when a news correspondent interviews a shy, unassuming Air Force Phantom jet fighter pilot in Southeast Asia in late 1967. So the correspondent wouldn't misconstrue the pilot's replies, the Wing Information Officer is on hand as a monitor to make certain that the real Air Force story would be told. The pilot was first asked his opinion of the F4C Phantom:

Captain: "It's so fuckin' maneuverable you can fly up your own ass with it."

IO: "What the captain means is that he has found the F4C Phantom highly maneuverable at all altitudes and he considers it an excellent aircraft for all missions assigned."

Corr.: "I suppose, captain, that you've flown a certain number of missions over North Vietnam. What did you think of the SAMs used by the North Vietnamese?"

Captain: "Why those bastards couldn't hit a bull in the ass with a bass fiddle. We fake the shit out of them. There's no sweat."

IO: "What the captain means is that the Surface-to-Air Missiles around Hanoi pose a serious problem to our air operations and that the pilots have a healthy respect for them."

Corr.: "I suppose, captain, that you've flown missions to the South. What kind of ordinance do you use, and what kind of targets do you hit?"

Captain: "Well, I'll tell you, mostly we aim at kicking the shit out of Vietnamese villages, and my favorite ordinance is napalm. Man, that stuff just sucks the air out of their friggin' lungs and makes a sonovabitchin' fire.

IO: "What the captain means is that air strikes in South Vietnam are often against Vietcong structures and all operations are always under the positive control of Forward Air Controllers, or FACs. The ordinance employed is conventional 500 and 750 pound bombs and 20 millimeter cannon fire.

Corr.: "I suppose you spent an R and R in Hong Kong. What were your impressions of the oriental girls?"

Captain: "Yeah, I went to Hong Kong. As for those oriental broads, well, I don't care which way the runway runs, east or west, north or south—a piece of ass is a piece of ass."

IO:	"What the captain means is that he found the delicately featured oriental girls fascinating, and he was very impressed with their fine manners and thinks their naiveté is most charming."
Corr.:	"Tell me, captain, have you flown any missions other than over North and South Vietnam?"
Captain:	"You bet your sweet ass I've flown other missions. We get scheduled nearly every day for a place where those fuckers over there throw everything at you but the friggin' kitchen sink. Even the goddam kids got slingshots.
IO:	"What the captain means is that he has occasionally been scheduled to fly missions in the extreme Western DMZ, and he has a healthy respect for the flak in that area."
Corr.:	"I understand that no one in your Fighter Wing has got a MIG yet. What seems to be the problem?"
Captain:	"Why you screwhead, if you knew anything about what you're talking about—the problem is MIGs. If we'd get scheduled by those peckerheads at Seventh for those missions in MIG Valley, you can bet your ass we'd get some of those mothers. Those glory hounds at Ubon get all those missions while we settle for fightin' the friggin war. Those mothers at Ubon are sitting on their fat asses killing MIGs and we get stuck with bombing the goddamned cabbage patches."
IO:	"What the captain means is that each element in the Seventh Air Force is responsible for doing their assigned job in the air war. Some units are assigned the job of neutralizing enemy air strength by hunting out MIGs, and other elements are assigned bombing missions and interdiction of enemy supply routes."
Corr.:	"Of all the targets you've hit in Vietnam, which one was the most satisfying?"
Captain:	"Well, shit, it was when we were scheduled for that suspected VC vegetable garden. I dropped napalm in the middle of the fuckin' cabbage and my wingman splashed it real good with six of those 750 pound mothers and spread the fire all the way to the friggin' beets and carrots."
IO:	"What the captain means is that the great variety of tactical targets available throughout Vietnam make the F4C the perfect aircraft to provide flexible response."

Corr.:	"What do you consider the most difficult target you've struck in North Vietnam?"
Captain:	"The friggin' bridges. I must have dropped 40 tons of bombs on those swayin' bamboo mothers, and I ain't hit one of the bastards yet."
IO:	What the captain means is that interdicting bridges along enemy supply routes is very important and a quite difficult target. The best way to accomplish this task is to crater the approaches to the bridge."
Corr.:	"I noticed in touring the base that you have aluminum matting on the taxiways. Would you care to comment on its effectiveness and usefulness in Vietnam?"
Captain:	"You're fuckin' right, I'd like to make a comment. Most of us pilots are well hung, but shit, you don't know what hung is until you get hung up on one of the friggin' bumps on that goddam stuff."
IO:	"What the captain means is that the aluminum matting is quite satisfactory as a temporary expedient, but required some finesse in taxiing and braking the aircraft."
Corr.:	"Did you have an opportunity to meet your wife on leave in Honolulu, and did you enjoy the visit with her?"
Captain:	Yeah, I met my wife in Honolulu, but I forgot to check the calendar, so the whole five days were friggin' well combat-proof—a completely dry run."
IO:	"What the captain means is that it was wonderful to get together with his wife and learn first-hand about the family and how things were at home."
Corr.:	"Thank you for your time, captain."
Captain:	"Screw you—why don't you bastards print the real story, instead of all that crap?"
IO:	"What the captain means is that he enjoyed the opportunity to discuss his tour with you."
Corr.:	"One final question. Could you reduce your impression of the war into a simple phrase or statement, captain?"
Captain:	"You bet your ass I can. It's a fucked up war."
IO:	"What the captain means is . . . It's a FUCKED UP WAR."

75. I Am Their Leader

In the military, there is great emphasis placed upon hierarchy and leadership. Leaders are expected to know what their men are doing and to keep tabs on them at all times. The following item collected in Walnut Creek, California, in 1991, demonstrates the opposite of the ideal.

Which way did they go?

How many were there?

How fast were they going?

I must find them

        I am their leader!

76. Welcome To...

When someone is lost, for example, driving an automobile, one looks for helpful road signs. Unfortunately, highways and roads are not always kept in good repair. Construction delays and/or detours are all too frequently encountered. No state is immune from these problems, as the following three texts attest. The first was collected in Chicago in 1994, the second from north central Pennsylvania in 1990, and the third from Las Vegas in mid-1994. While demonstrating considerable variation, the three versions are definitely cognate. Most states have judiciously placed large welcome signs at their borders boasting of the state's principal attractions. This item parodies such greetings with a warning of road impediments and problems likely to be encountered en route.

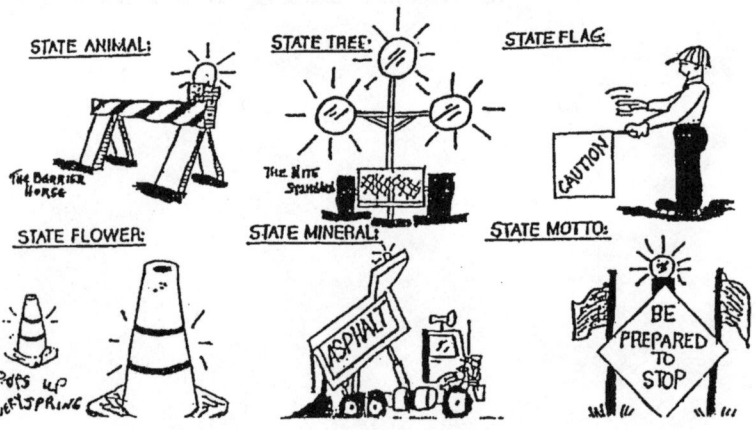

WELCOME TO PENNSYLVANIA
THE STATE WHERE EVERY HIGHWAY EVENTUALLY NARROWS TO A SINGLE LANE OR IS DETOURED

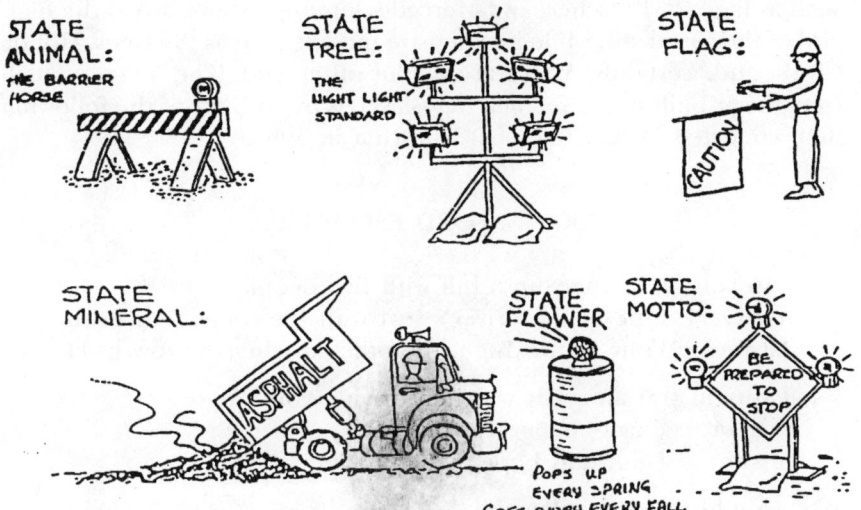

Welcome to Nevada ...
THE STATE WHERE EVERY STREET EVENTUALLY NARROWS TO A SINGLE LANE OR IS ...

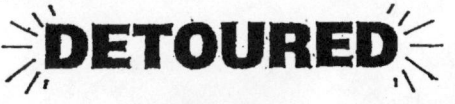

DETOURED

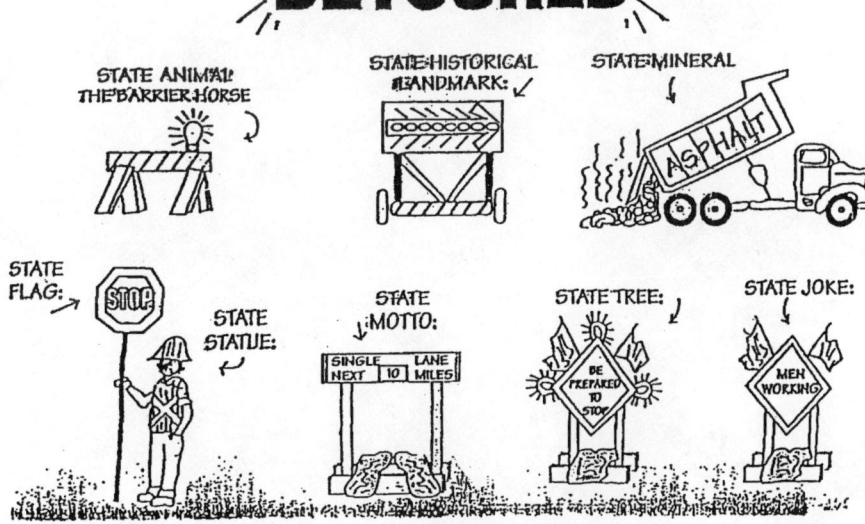

77. Yugo's, Ford Escorts, . . .

American automobile culture includes a definite hierarchy. Luxury cars such as Jaguars, Porsches, and Mercedes, among others, are at the high end of the spectrum, while inexpensive models such as the Geos, Honda Civics, and, certainly, Yugos are at the other end. The Yugo, a small foreign car built in the former Yugoslavia, is the subject of the following item collected in San Ramon, California in 1993.

YUGO'S, FORD ESCORTS, . . .

How do you get a Yugo up a hill with five people?
   Answer 1: One in the driver's seat with the other four pushing.
   Answer 2: Four in the Yugo, the other driving the tow truck.

What should you always have when driving your Yugo?
   Answer 1: Exact change for bus fare.
   Answer 2: Faith and hope.

Why should you buy a Yugo?
   Answer 1: So you appreciate other cars.
   Answer 2: So that you'll always have an excuse for being late.

How do you double the value of a Yugo? Fill it with gas.

78. Van Gogh's Family

Vincent van Gogh (1853–1890) is a celebrated Dutch painter who was virtually unknown during his lifetime. The pronunciation of his name in Dutch would not provide the necessary punning basis for the following item, the first version of which was collected in Lafayette, California, in February 1999, and the second version in Berkeley in March 1998. The item depends upon pronouncing "Gogh" as "go."

VINCENT VAN GOGH'S FAMILY

Even the most ardent art aficionados might not know that Vincent Van Gogh had a really large family. I have discovered some of his lesser known relatives recently while surfing on line:

- His grandfather who moved to Yugoslavia . . . U. Gogh
- His great-great grandniece who wore miniskirts and liked to dance . . . Go Gogh
- His real obnoxious brother . . . Please Gogh
- His uncle who worked in a convenience store . . . Stop N. Gogh
- His dizzy sister . . . Verti Gogh
- His brother who ate prunes . . . Gotta Gogh
- His cousin who moved to Illinois . . . Chica Gogh
- His uncle the magician . . . Wherediddy Gogh
- His cousin that lived in Mexico . . . Amee Gogh
- His grandson living in North Dakota . . . Far Gogh
- His nephew who drove a stage coach . . . Wells Far Gogh
- His aunt who loved ballroom dancing . . . Tan Gogh
- His uncle the ornithologist . . . Flamin Gogh
- His cousin the astrologer . . . Vir Gogh
- His nephew, the Freudian psychoanalyst . . . E. Gogh
- His feminist activist daughter Mary who retained her maiden name after marrying Thomas Round . . . Mary Go-Round
- His beatnik uncle with the clipped beard . . . Gogh, T.
- His beach bum nephew in Florida . . . Key Lar Gogh
- His son the commercial advertising artist . . . Lo Gogh
- His brother-in-law the stevedore . . . Car Gogh
- His Italian cousin . . . De Gogh

After much careful research it has been discovered that the artist Vincent Van Gogh had many relatives. Among them were:

His obnoxious brother . . . . Please Gogh
His dizzy aunt . . . . Verti Gogh
The brother who ate prunes . . . . Gotta Gogh
The brother who worked at a convenience store . . . . Stopn Gogh
The grandfather from Yugoslavia . . . . U Gogh
The brother who bleached his clothes white . . . . Hue Gogh
The cousin from Illinois . . . . Chica Gogh
His magician uncle . . . . Wherediddy Gogh
His Mexican cousin . . . . Amee Gogh
The Mexican cousin's American half brother . . . . Grin Gogh
The nephew who drove a stage coach . . . . Wellsfar Gogh
The constipated uncle . . . . Cant Gogh
The ballroom dancing aunt . . . . Tan Gogh
The bird lover uncle . . . . Flamin Gogh
His nephew psychoanalyst . . . . E. Gogh
The fruit loving cousin . . . . Man Gogh
An aunt who taught positive thinking . . . . Way to Gogh
The little bouncy nephew . . . . Poe Gogh
A sister who loved disco . . . . Go Gogh
His Italian uncle . . . . Day Gogh
And his niece who travels the country in a van . . . Winnie Bay Gogh

A different text similarly puns on the name Van Gogh as well as the names of other painters. It was collected in Berkeley in August of 1999.

```
Subject: art theft

Recently a guy in Paris nearly got away with stealing several paintings
from the Louvre.

However, after planning the crime, breaking in, evading security, getting
out and escaping with the goods, he was captured only two blocks away when
his Econoline van ran out of gas.

When asked how he could mastermind such a crime and then make such an
obvious error, he replied:

"I had no Monet to buy Degas to make the Van Gogh."
```

79. Actual Advertisements

Americans are bombarded with advertisements—on the radio, on television, in newspapers and magazines, in movie theaters, and on billboards. Some advertisements are prepared by professional ad agencies, but others are composed by individuals for the classified sections of local newspapers. Typographical errors, misplaced modifiers and other mistakes sometimes afford unintentional humor. The following text collected in Santa Ana, California, in 1996, claims to be a list of genuine advertisements.

ACTUAL ADVERTISEMENTS

- Lost: small apricot poodle. Reward. Neutered. Like one of the family.
- A superb and inexpensive restaurant. Fine food expertly served by waitresses in appetizing forms.
- Dinner Special—Turkey $2.35; Chicken or Beef $2.25; Children $2.00.
- For sale: an antique desk suitable for lady with thick legs and large drawers.
- Four-poster bed, 101 years old. Perfect for antique lover.
- We do not tear your clothing with machinery. We do it carefully by hand.
- Dog for sale: eats anything and is fond of children.
- Vacation Special: have your home exterminated.
- Mt. Kilimanjaro, the breathtaking backdrop for the Serena Lodge. Swim in the lovely pool while you drink it all in.
- The hotel has bowling alleys, tennis courts, comfortable beds, and other athletic facilities.
- Stock up and save. Limit: one.
- Man wanted to work in dynamite factory. Must be willing to travel.
- Used Cars: Why go elsewhere to be cheated? Come here first!
- Christmas tag-sale. Handmade gifts for the hard-to-find person.
- Our bikinis are exciting. They are simply the tops.
- Illiterate? Write today for free help.
- Girl wanted to assist magician in cutting-off-head illusion. Blue Cross and salary.

Another version from Santa Ana in 1992 (not presented here) contains such additional entries as:

Tired of cleaning yourself? Let me do it.

Save regularly in our bank. You'll never reget it.

Wanted: chambermaid in rectory. Love in, $200 month. References required.

3-year-old teacher needed for pre-school. Experience preferred.

Auto Repair Service. Free pickup and delivery. Try us once, you'll never go anywhere again.

Wanted: Preparer of food. Must be dependable, like food business, and be willing to get hands dirty.

Semi-Annual after-Christmas Sale.

And now, the superstore—unequaled in size, unmatched in variety unrivaled inconvenience.

80. The Passing of the Energizer Bunny

One of the long-running commercials on American television advertises a battery by showing a moving pink toy bunny beating a drum. The implication is that the battery never wears out and that the bunny will go on forever. However, in the folk reaction to this commercial, it is quite another aspect of rabbits that is celebrated. Rabbits are associated with unbridled reproductive activity as the following obituary notice illustrates. It was collected in Berkeley, California in 1996. For another text based on similar wordplay, see NLM, 904.

I'm saddened to announce the passing of the Energizer Bunny.

<<AP August 22, 1996—the Energizer Bunny, known best for "going and going and going..." passed away last evening at 12:42 a.m.

Upon completion of the autopsy early this morning, the chief medical examiner ruled that the death was caused by acute cardiac arrest, induced by sexual over-stimulation.

Apparently, someone put the battery in backwards and the bunny kept coming and coming and coming...

Foul play has not been ruled out.

A second version which includes the outline of a rabbit in the form of a computer-generated graphic was collected via e-mail in San Francisco in 1999.

The Energizer Bunny

Tragic News to report. Please do not let this upset you too much.

Today, the world was stunned by the news of the death of the Energizer Bunny. He was six years old. Authorities believe that the death occurred at approximately 8:42 last evening. Best known as the irritating pink bunny that kept going, and going, and going, "Pinkie", as he was known to his friends and family, was alone at the time of his death. An emergency autopsy was performed early this morning. Chief Medical Examiner, Dura Cell, concluded that the cause of death was acute cardiac arrest induced by sexual over-stimulation. Apparently, someone had put the bunny's batteries in backwards and he kept coming, and coming, and coming...

81. What Is This?

If the Energizer Bunny has the capacity to keep going, and going, and going, so also are there individuals who would like to think that they have done likewise. In the following bit of braggadocio, which culminates in a complaint, we have a veritable litany of hardships that, however, pale in comparison to the present situation, whatever that may be. The first version was collected in Riverside, California, in March 1995, while the second was collected in Downsville, New York in mid-1996. For other versions, see FOJ, 147, UOH, 50.

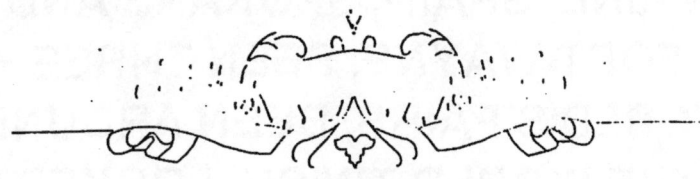

What Is This?

*I've seen Wars, Rebellions, Riots and other minor personality clashes; I've fought fires and floods and have been scared shitless by earthquakes; I've seen muggings, robberies, killings, and other small discourtesies, I've had (and been had by) some women, good, bad and average; I've been confused, amused, abused, confounded, dumbfounded and otherwise shook-up; I've been run off, laid off, fired, thrown out and even politely dismissed; I've smoked rope, chewed dope and seen goats fuck in the market-place; But **I AIN'T NEVER SEEN NO SHIT LIKE THIS***

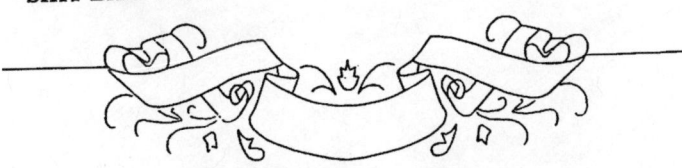

I'VE SMOKED DOPE, CHEWED ROPE, DANCED, FRENCH-ROMANCED, FUCKED, FARTED, FOUGHT, SHOT THE MOON, DROVE BIG TRUCKS;
I'VE BEEN TO JANESVILLE, MAINE, SPAIN, SPOKANE AND FORT WAYNE, SEEN THREE WORLD'S FAIRS, BEEN AROUND THE WORLD TWICE, LOOKED DANGER IN THE FACE, SEEN GOATS FUCK IN THE MARKETPLACE, BUT I AIN'T NEVER SEEN NO SHIT LIKE THE SHIT THAT GOES ON AROUND THIS PLACE!

From the Funny File

Of all the thousands upon thousands of orally transmitted jokes, only a relatively small percentage succeed in making the transition to photocopier tradition. This percentage includes lists of one-liners belonging to a particular joke cycle, e.g., blonde or dumb men jokes. Such lists transmitted via e-mail or the Internet frequently are cumulative in nature, resulting in would-be "complete" or "definitive" compilations. In the case of extended series, it is extremely unlikely that all of the texts included would be recounted in any one oral performance.

In view of the limited number of oral jokes that surface in copier form, one is tempted to speculate as to why some jokes do so while most others do not. Presumably, the selection process might provide a clue as to the folk judgement regarding which texts are deemed especially relevant to current issues or are considered to be esthetically superior. The following texts constitute a representative sampling of those jokes that are to be found in photocopier tradition.

82. Please Divert Your Course

There is an idiom in American folk speech which aptly describes an impasse, namely, "When an irresistible force meets an immovable object." This situation can also provide the basis for humor. The following text, collected from Alumni House on the University of California, Berkeley campus in January 1996, encapsulates the authoritarianism often associated with hierarchical rank in the military. A second version from Wilmington, Delaware, reported in December of 1999, features Canadians and Americans as protagonists. In an oral version from the 1970s, the confrontation is heightened by the captain of a battleship interacting with a seaman deuce, the lowest enlisted grade in the U.S. Navy. For another version, see Karen Warner, *500 Great Bartender's Jokes* (New York: Penguin, 1993), 198.

Actual radio conversation released by
the Chief of Naval Operations, 10-10-95.

Station #1: Please divert your course 15 degrees to the North to avoid a collision.

Station #2: Recommend you divert YOUR course 15 degrees to South to avoid a collision.

#1: This is the Captain of a US Navy ship. I say again, divert YOUR course.

#2: No. I say again, you divert YOUR course.

#1: THIS IS THE AIRCRAFT CARRIER ENTERPRISE, WE ARE A LARGE WARSHIP OF THE US NAVY. DIVERT YOUR COURSE NOW!

#2: This is the Puget Sound lighthouse. It's your call.

More Embarrassing Moments

This is the transcript of an ACTUAL dialogue between the US Navy and.....well, you'll see.

The moral of the story...tis better to be thought a fool than to open your moth and prove it!

Americans: Please divert your course 15 degrees to the North to avoid a collision.

Canadians: Recommend you divert YOUR course 15 degrees to the South to avoid a collision.

Americans: This is the Captain of a US Navy ship. I say again, divert YOUR course.

Canadians: No. I say again, you divert YOUR course.

Americans: THIS IS THE AIRCRAFT CARRIER USS LINCOLN, THE SECOND LARGEST SHIP IN THE UNITED STATES' ATLANTIC FLEET. WE ARE ACCOMPANIED BY THREE DESTROYERS, THREE CRUISERS AND NUMEROUS SUPPORT VESSELS.

I DEMAND THAT YOU CHANGE YOUR COURSE 15 DEGREES NORTH, THAT'S ONE FIVE DEGREES NORTH, OR COUNTER-MEASURES WILL BE UNDERTAKEN TO ENSURE THE SAFETY OF THIS SHIP.

Canadians: This is a lighthouse. Your call.

83. Mad Dogs and Englishmen

When a military officer makes a mistake, he can be sure that it will be duly noted in his periodic evaluation or "fitness report." An officer's career may be seriously impacted by either a slightly negative or even a neutral or restrained review by his immediate superior. The following item was reported in San Francisco in November 1996. Although it refers specifically to the British Royal Navy, it could in theory apply to the military personnel of any nation. The title comes from a phrase in a 1931 song composed by Noel Coward. The full line is "Mad dogs and Englishmen/Go out in the midday sun." In another version from San Francisco in 1999 (not presented here) titled "Actual Quotes from Federal Employee Evaluations," we find the following additional descriptions: "A gross ignoramus—144 times worse than an ordinary ignoramus," "If you see two people talking and one looks bored, he's the other one," and "If you give him a penny for his thoughts, you'd get change." For other photocopier treatments of fitness reports and employee evaluations, see NT, 28–31.

MAD DOGS AND ENGLISHMEN

The British Military writes OFR's (officer fitness reports). The form used for Royal Navy and Marines fitness reports is the S206.

The following are actual excerpts taken from people's "206's"...

- His men would follow him anywhere, but only out of curiosity.
- I would not breed from this Officer.
- This Officer is really not so much of a has-been, but more of a definitely won't be.
- When she opens her mouth, it seems that this is only to change whichever foot was previously in there.
- He has carried out each and every one of his duties to his entire satisfaction.
- He would be out of his depth in a car park puddle.
- Technically sound, but socially impossible.
- This Officer reminds me very much of a gyroscope—always spinning around at a frantic pace, but not really going anywhere.

- This young lady has delusions of adequacy.
- When he joined my ship, this Officer was something of a granny; since then he has aged considerably.
- This Medical Officer has used my ship to carry his genitals from port to port, and my officers to carry him from bar to bar.
- Since my last report he has reached rock bottom, and has started to dig.
- She sets low personal standards and then consistently fails to achieve them.
- He has the wisdom of youth, and the energy of old age.
- This Officer should go far—and the sooner he starts, the better.
- In my opinion this pilot should not be authorized to fly below 250 feet.
- The only ship I would recommend this man for is citizenship.
- Works well when under constant supervision and cornered like a rat in a trap.
- This man is depriving a village somewhere of an idiot.

84. Honk If You Love Jesus

Jokes can be very complex and involve a multitude of themes. In the following text, collected in Barboursville, Virginia, in March 1996, we find an illustration of such complexity. There is a parody of simplistic religious fervor as reflected in bumper sticker mottoes. There is a pointed commentary on the frustration of individuals in traffic who are being unnecessarily impeded by an inattentive or incompetent driver. Above all, there is a marked contrast between the naive innocence of the narrator and the vulgar words and gestures of the angry inconvenienced motorists. The incredible misperception of such common insults as the digitus impudicus (e.g., "the finger" [cf. WH, 154, WY, 186–91]) adds to the comic effect. Although the gender of the narrator is not indicated, it could be argued that it is a woman, not a man, the implication being that most males would immediately recognize the gestures or obscenities all too often encountered in everyday life. In this context, there may be an allusion to the stereotype of a "woman driver," referring to the alleged lack of driving skill of women, and perhaps to the notion that women tend to be more devoutly religious than men, and to the convention that mothers—not fathers—drive children to and from school or other activities. In this text, even the children appear to know more about obscene gestures than their benighted mother.

The other day I went to the local religious book store, where I saw a HONK IF YOU LOVE JESUS bumper sticker. I bought it and put it on the back bumper of my car, and I'm really glad I did. What an uplifting experience followed!

I was stopped at the light at a busy intersection, just lost in thought about the Lord, and didn't notice that the light had changed. That bumper sticker really worked! I found lots of people who love Jesus.

Why, the guy behind me started to honk like crazy. He must REALLY love the Lord because pretty soon, he leaned out his window and yelled, "Jesus Christ!" as loud as he could. It was like a football game with him shouting, "GO JESUS CHRIST, GO!"

Everyone else started honking, too, so I leaned out my window and waved and smiled to all of those loving people.

There must have been a guy from Florida back there because I could hear him yelling something about a sunny beach, and saw him waving in a funny way with only his middle finger stuck up in the air.

I asked my two kids what that meant. They kind of squirmed, looked at each other, giggled and told me that it was the Hawaiian good luck sign. So, I leaned out the window and gave him the good luck sign back.

Several cars behind, a very nice black man stepped out of his car and yelled something. I couldn't hear him very well, but it sounded like, "Mother trucker," or "Mother's from there." Maybe he was from Florida, too. He must really love the Lord.

A couple of the people were so caught up in the joy of the moment that they got out of their cars and were walking toward me. I bet they wanted to pray, but just then I noticed that the light had changed to yellow, and stepped on the gas.

And a good thing I did, because I was the only driver to get across the intersection. I looked back at them standing there. I leaned way out the window, gave them a big smile and held up the Hawaiian good luck sign as I drove away.

Praise the Lord for such wonderful folks.

85. Schnauzer

Verbal misunderstandings are by no means the exclusive property of women. Men too are capable of gross misinterpretations. In the following text from Iselin, New Jersey, collected in February 1992, it is the male druggist who mistakenly assumed that an unfamiliar word refers to a female body part. The joke also depends upon the implicit sexual significance of hair and the removal thereof. For discussions of hair symbolism, see Aug. Gittée, "Les Cheveux dans l'Enthnographie et le Folk-Lore," *Revue des Traditions Populaires 3* (1888), 401–06; Charles Berg, *The Unconcious Significance of Hair* (London: George Allen & Unwin, 1951); Edmund R. Leach, "Magical Hair," *Journal of the Royal Anthropological Institute* 88 (1958), 147–64; and Gananath Obeyesekere, *Medusa's Hair* (Chicago, Univ. of Chicago Press, 1981). For other photocopier treatments of female pubic hair, see WY, 136, and SD 240–42.

Concerned about her Schnauzer's inability to move its head for the last several days, Mrs. Jones brought her dog to the local vet's office to resolve the problem. Upon examination, the vet assured Mrs. Jones the problem was caused by poor grooming habits and could be corrected by cutting the hair on the Schnauzer's ears and neck. After cutting the dog's hair the vet suggested that Nair, a depilatory, be applied to the dog's ears once a month to prevent a reoccurrence of the problem. After paying the bill, Mrs. Jones brought the dog home and drove to the nearest druggist to purchase a bottle of Nair. Upon returning with the item requested, the druggist asked Mrs. Jones if she had ever used this product before. She replied "NO!" the druggist then went on to explain that if she applied the product to her underarms, she should wait two or three hours before putting on a blouse because it might stain her blouse or cause skin irritation. Likewise, if she was to apply it to her legs, she should wait two or three hours before putting on tights or pantyhose because it could stain her garments and cause skin irritation. The woman responded that she was not going to apply the Nair to her underarms or her legs, she was going to put it on her Schnauzer. The druggist, with a bewildered look on his face, replied "OH! . . . , in that case, I recommend that you don't ride a bike for at least two or three days."

86. You Read It Here First

The male misunderstanding of female anatomy is also featured in the following text collected in Chicago in December 1983. The American Puritan heritage continues to manifest itself in a prudishness about bodily functions and sexuality. Even in modern so-called enlightened times, men may be embarrassed to ask female sales clerks for condoms and women may be equally embarrassed to ask male salesclerks for feminine hygiene products. According to one feminist-inspired argument, the very taboo status of menstruation is attributable to male efforts to demonstrate female inferiority. See Sophie Laws, *Issues of Blood: The Politics of Menstruation* (London: Macmillan, 1990), 28–31. The sadistic nuances of the punchline of the test would tend to confirm the feminist hypothesis.

YOU READ IT HERE FIRST

Our source claims that the following incident is 100 percent true fact. We are reserving final judgment until we can obtain signed and notarized affidavits from each participant, a tape recording of the entire proceedings and a clear eight-by-ten glossy photograph of the premises. Meanwhile, you make up your own minds.

In Tucson, Arizona, a newspaper reporter wandered into a large discount department store to spend some money. The reporter wound up in a check-out line behind an empty-handed woman who, when she got to the checker, explained that she had not been able to find the item she was after on the shelves. "What was it you wanted, ma'am?" the check-out girl asked.
"Tampax."

"What kind?" the girl asked.
"Super."
So the check-out girl got on the microphone at her station and blurted over the store-wide intercom: "Stockboy, we need a box of super Tampax right away at register seven."
The woman went crimson but stood her ground.
But the stockboy didn't hear the mes'sage clearly--he thought the checker had called for thumbtacks. So he shouted from the back of the store: "Do you want the kind you push in with your finger or the ones you pound in with a hammer?"

87. We Could Have Saved the Bentley

According to the late Gershon Legman (1917–1999), the authority on sexual folklore, "The commonest insult concerning the female genitals is that they are too big" (RDJ, 377). The following text, collected in Walnut Creek, California, in February 1988, exemplifies this theme. Legman traces the joke, which typically refers to saving a horse and wagon rather than a car, back at least to a poeticized version dating from 1735 (RDJ, 378). If we consider this date a terminus ante quem, that would make this item at least two hundred and fifty years old. The earlier texts do refer to hiding jewelry as does the updated text presented here. This text also plays upon an all-too-familiar theme of exposing the alleged scandals of the "Royals" in England. In this context, the members of the royal family themselves become subjects to be endlessly exploited by the tabloid press. Presumably Princess Margaret's alleged sexual escapades account for her role in the punchline. The theme of the oversized vagina is also featured in folksong. An obvious example is "Three Old Whores," where three women successively brag about the excessive size of their vaginas. See G. Legman, *The Horn Book: Studies in Erotic Folklore and Bibliography* (New Hyde Park: Univ. Books, 1964), 414, where he claims that the song is "the oldest surviving erotic folksong in English." See also Ed Cray, *The Erotic Muse* (New York: Oak Publications, 1969), 191–93, 2nd edition (Urbana: Univ. Illinois Press, 1992), 6–11; and Vance Randolph, *Roll Me in Your Arms: "Unprintable" Ozark Folksongs and Folklore,* Vol. I (Fayetteville: Univ. of Arkansas Press, 1992), 121–23.

Queen Elizabeth and Lady Di are out for a drive in the royal car on a Sunday afternoon, and they slow down when they see a man by the roadside signaling for help. But no sooner has the car come to a stop than he springs to the door, pulls out a gun, and orders them both out of the car. "Queen Elizabeth" he snarls, "hand over that snazzy diamond tiara you're always wearing."

"I'm terribly sorry, my good man," says the queen, "but I'm afraid I don't wear it on Sundays."

"Aw, hell," says the guy. "Well listen, Di, hand over that fancy engagement ring I keep seeing in all the pictures."

"I'm terribly sorry," says Lady Di sweetly, "but I'm afraid I didn't put it on this morning. It must still be on my night table."

"Aw, shit," growls the guy. " I guess I'll just grab the car." So off he drives at the wheel of the Bentley, leaving the two woman walking down the road in the direction of London. After a few minutes have passed, Lady Di asks the queen, "Pardon my curiosity, Your Highness, but I'm quite sure you had that tiara on this morning. Didn't you?"

"Indeed I did," confesses the queen, blushing slightly and pointing. "I hid it... down there. And you, Diana, weren't you wearing your ring?"

Yes she had been, says Diana, turning beet red, and she had resorted to the same hiding place.

They walked a few more steps in companionable silence when Queen Elizabeth lets out a little sigh. "I do wish Princess Margaret had been with us," she says. "We could have saved the Bentley."

88. Another Wife Story

If one supposed complaint of a husband is that his wife's vagina is too large, a far more common grievance is the wife's refusal to grant him access to it. From a male perspective, the wife's indifference is used as a rationalization for infidelity. (For another photocopier treatment of the wife's alleged refusal to engage in sexual activity, see WH 16–18.) The following text was collected in Chicago in 1994.

ANOTHER WIFE STORY

A wife arriving home after shopping was horrified to find her husband in bed with a pretty young thing. Just as she was about to storm out of the house, her husband stopped her with these words:

"Before you leave, I want you to hear how this all came about. I was driving along the highway when I saw this young girl looking very tired and bedraggled, so I offered her a lift. She was hungry, so I brought her home and made her a meal from the roast you had forgotten in the refrigerator. She had only worn sandals on her feet, so I gave her a pair of good shoes you had discarded because they were out of style. She was cold, so I gave her the sweater I bought for your birthday—the one you never wore because you said the colors didn't suit you. Her slacks were pretty well worn out too, so I gave her a pair of yours that were perfectly good, but have become too small for you. Then, as she was about to leave the house, she paused and asked "Is there anything else your wife doesn't use anymore?"

89. Game Time

The flip side of the male's complaint about oversized female genitalia is the supposed female unhappiness with the inadequate size of the male sexual organ. We say "supposed" because it is quite likely that it is more often males, not females, who are extremely concerned about penis size. As G. Legman observes, "Rather than admit that the penis is "too small" as is fearfully believed, it is far simpler to state that the vagina is "too big" (RDJ, 377). The following text, collected in New York City in December 1989, depicts a put-down in sporting terms. For earlier versions from 1945 and 1953, with an additional husband's retort referring to watermelons or grapefruits, see RDJ, 539.

GAME TIME

His wife accompanied him on the business trip against his wishes, but after dinner in a fine restaurant and a pleasant evening at the theater, his mood had mellowed, and he almost felt amiable when they arrived back at their hotel room. He glanced out the window and happened to see a couple across the air shaft. His attention became riveted.

"George, what are you doing, George?" whined his wife, a perennial whiner.

"I'm looking at the couple across the air shaft."

"George, what are they doing, George?"

"As best I can tell, he's trying to pitch grapes into her snatch, and she's trying ring-a-rosy-oh with doughnuts on his dick. Want to give it a try?"

"Sure, George, sure. Pass me the lifesavers."

90. Chinese Torture Test

The main fear of sexual inadequacy is exceeded only by the threat of castration. There are countless jokes devoted to this theme (cf. NLM 420–671; for photocopier examples, see NT 394–400, SD 203–12). The following text was collected by a twenty-two year old Chinese-American male in February 1996 on the University of California, Berkeley, campus. For another version with no Chinese reference, see NLM, 808–09.

Once there was a man that survived a terrible plane crash and was lost in a forest. . . . He had no idea where he was or which way to go. He wandered for days and survived on berries and twigs. After two weeks of wandering he found a small two story house with smoke coming out of the chimney. He quickly knocked on the door.

A small Chinese man answered the door.
"Please I need some food and shelter," said the young man.
"This I will give you but you must promise not to fool with my lovely daughter." The old man said.
"Thank you and I wouldn't think of messing with your daughter."
"For if you do I will inflict the Three Chinese Torture Test."
He agreed again and entered the man's house.
After some sleep and a bath, a dinner was set up and the man sat to eat. The old man's daughter entered the room and to the surprise of the young man, she was the most beautiful woman he's ever seen. Remember, he's been out in the wilderness for some time now. She was so beautiful he could hardly keep from staring at her throughout dinner.
Later that night the man crept into the girl's room just to take one last look at her, for he promised to leave early the next morning. He opened the door and saw the girl awake, and to his surprise she asked him in. They were as quiet at possible not to wake the old man and after a few hours the man crept to his room thinking any torture would be worth what he's just had. So he went to sleep happy.
He woke up in the morning and felt a great pain on his chest. It was a rock with a sign on it. It said:
1st Chinese torture, 100 pound rock on chest!
Well, this wasn't anything, so he threw the rock out the window. As he did this he saw a second sign on the back of the rock and it said:
2nd Chinese torture test, Left testicle tied to 100 pound rock.
The man without hesitation jumped out of the window, and as he fell he saw a large sign on the ground, it said:
3rd Chinese torture, Right Testicle tied to bed post.

91. How'd You Break Your Arm?

Another potential source of embarrassment involving the sexual organs concerns urination and excretion. In American society, such acts are normally very private ones. On the other hand, there are times and places when toilet facilities are not readily available and individuals must relieve themselves as best they can. The following text articulates the common fear that one may be observed in a compromising situation and exposed for all the world to see. It was collected in Walnut Creek, California in 1994.

HOW'D YOU BREAK YOUR ARM?

A friend just got back from a holiday ski trip to Utah where the conditions were perfect—12 below, no feeling in the toes, basic numbness all over, and a "tell me when we're having fun" kind of day.

One of the women in the group complained to her husband that she was in dire need of a rest room. He told her not to worry, that he was sure there was relief waiting at the top of the lift in the form of a powder room for female skiers in distress. He was wrong, of course, and the pain did not go away.

If you've ever had nature hit its panic button in you, then you know that a temperature of 12 below zero doesn't help matters. So, with time running out, the women weighed her options. Her husband picked up on the intensity of the pain and suggested that since she was wearing an all-white ski outfit, she should go off into the woods. No one would even notice, he assured her. The white would provide more than adequate camouflage. So she headed for the tree line, began disrobing and proceeded to do her thing.

If you've ever parked on the side of a slope, then you know there is a right way and a wrong way to "set" your skies so you don't move. Yup, you got it. She had them positioned wrong. Steep slopes are not forgiving, even during embarrassing moments. Without warning, the woman found herself skiing backward, out of control, racing through the trees, somehow missing all of them, and onto another slope. Her derriere and the reverse side were still bare, her pants down around her knees, and she was picking up speed all the while. She continued on backward, totally out of control, creating an unusual vista for other skiers.

The woman skied, if you define the term loosely, back under the lift, and finally collided violently with a pylon. The bad news was that she broke her arm and was unable to pull up her ski pants. At long last her husband arrived, put an end to her embarrassment, then went to the base of the mountain and summoned the ski patrol, who transported her to the hospital.

In the emergency room she was regrouping when a man with an obviously broken leg was put in the bed next to hers. "So how'd you break your leg?" she asked, making small talk.

"It was the darnedest thing you ever saw," he said. "I was riding up the ski lift, and suddenly I couldn't believe my eyes. There was this crazy woman skiing backward out of control down the mountain with her bare bottom hanging out of her clothes and her pants down around her knees. I leaned over to get a better look and I guess I didn't realize how far I'd moved. I fell out of the ski lift." "—So, how'd you break your arm?"

92. Blondes

Within the framework of male stereotypes of females, there is a particular set of jokes featuring "dumb blondes." In popular culture too, one finds frequent illustrations of this stereotype, e.g., the comic strip "Blondie" and such actresses as Judy Holiday and Marilyn Monroe. It is possible that the renewed circulation of blond jokes may be attributed to a male reaction to the feminist (or women's) liberation-movement. In any case, blond jokes continue to be told, most often presumably, by men. They may be individual texts, or they may appear as a list of one-liners. The most prominent traits of the blond stereotype are empty-headedness and sexual promiscuity.

The first illustrative text was collected from a Hewlett-Packard facility in Sunnyvale, California in 1996; the second from a Catholic High School in Hayward, California in 1994; the third from Greensburg, Pennyslvania in 1997; and the fourth, a list of blonde jokes, was collected in Northridge, California in 1996. With respect to the list, some of the jokes are new, but many are recycled from earlier traditions, e.g., the Polish-American jokes. For an anthology of blonde jokes, see Blanche Knott, *Truly Tasteless Blonde Jokes* (New York: St. Martin's Press, 1992). For discussion, see Jeannie B. Thomas, "Dumb Blondes, Dan Quayle, and Hillary Clinton: Gender, Sexuality, and Stupidity in Jokes," *Journal of American Folklore* 110 (1997), 277–313.

A blonde girl boarded a plane and sat herself in first class.
The stewardess came over and told her she couldn't sit there.
The blonde said, "I'm blonde, I'm beautiful, and I'm very intelligent. I'll stay here until we reach Chicago."
The stewardess tells her that she didn't pay for first class and she has to move.
The blonde says the same thing, "I'm blonde, I'm beautiful, and I'm very intelligent. I'll stay here until we reach Chicago.
The stewardess is really frustrated so she goes to the head stewardess.
The head stewardess tells the blonde that she has to move.
But the blonde woman says the same thing, "I'm blonde, I'm beautiful, and I'm very intelligent. I'll stay here until we reach Chicago."
They finally call the co-pilot over. They explain the situation to him.
The co-pilot whispers something in the blonde's ear, and she gets up and leaves.
Both stewardesses are amazed; they ask him what he said to make her leave.
He says, "Well, I just told her that first class doesn't fly to Chicago."

A blonde walks into a pizza parlor.
She says she wants to order a large pizza.
The pizza maker asks her, "Do you want that cut into 12 pieces or 24?"
The blonde says, "I could never eat 24 pieces!"

A group of blondes walk into a bar. One of them tells the bartender to line up a row of drinks for all of them. They lift their glasses and toast.
   "Here's to 51 days!" and they proceed to down their drinks.
   Once again, they tell the bartender to "line 'em up" and once again they toast 51 days and down their drinks...
   The bartender says, "I don't get it. Why in the world are you toasting 51 days?"
   One of the blondes explains, "We just finished a jigsaw puzzle that had 2–4 years written on the box, and we finished it in 51 days."

BLONDES

Q: Why do blondes like tilt steering?
A: It gives them more head room.

Q: Why do blondes wear shoulder pads?
A: So they won't hurt themselves when they say, "I don't know."

Q: How do you make a blond's eyes sparkle?
A: Shine a flashlight in her ear.

Q: How do you make a blonde laugh on Monday?
A: Tell her a joke on Friday.

Q: What does a blonde say after sex?
A: "Who are you guys?"

Q: How does a blonde turn on the lights after sex?
A: She opens the car door.

Q: How do you change a blonde's mind?
A: Blow in her ear.

Q: What's the similarity between a blonde and a turtle?
A: Once on their backs, they are both screwed.

Q: Why do blondes wear panties?
A: To keep their ankles warm.

Q: What's the first thing a blonde does after sex?
A: Goes home.

Q: Why do blondes have T.G.I.F. painted on their shoes?
A: To remind them that "Toes go in first."

Q: Whats the similarity between Santa Claus, the tooth fairy, and a smart blonde?
A: They are all make-believe.

Q: What's the similarity between blondes and computers?
A: No one appreciates them 'til they go down on you.

Q: What's the difference between a blonde and a limousine?
A: Not everyone has been in a limousine.

Q: Why will a blonde laugh at a joke three times?
A: Once when you tell it, once when you tell her the punch line, and once when she gets it.

Q: What's the mating call of a blonde?
A: Take me home, I'm drunk.

Q: What's the difference between a blonde and trampoline?
A: You take your shoes off before you get on a trampoline.

Q: Why don't blondes like vibrators?
A: They are too hard on their teeth.

Q: What do you call a blonde who has dyed her hair black?
A: Artificial intelligence.

Q: What is the similarity between cowpies and blondes?
A: The older they get, the easier they are to pick up.

Q: Why don't blondes eat pickles?
A: They can't get their heads in the jars.

Q: What's the difference between a blonde and the Suez Canal?
A: One is the busy ditch!

Q: Why did the blonde get fired from the "M" & "M" factory?
A: Because she kept throwing out the "Ws"!

Q: What does a blonde wear around her ears to make her look sexy?
A: Her legs!!

Q: Why does a blonde spike her hair?
A: So the jokes won't go over her head.

Q: Why does a blonde sit in front of a fan with her mouth open every three days?
A: To recharge.

Among the jokes included on other lists (not presented here) are:

What did the dumb blonde name her pet Zebra? Spot.

Why don't blondes like to make Kool-Aid (Jello)? Because they can't fit two quarts of water into the package.

What do blondes say after making love? Are you boys all on the same team?

What does a blond say after multiple orgasms? "Way to go team!"

Why did God give blondes one more brain cell than a horse? So when they're waving in a parade, they won't crap in the street.

What do you say to a blonde with no arms and no legs? "Nice tits!"

What do you call a smart blonde? A golden retriever.

One interesting offshoot of the blonde joke cycle is an apparent sequel involving put-downs of brunettes. A number of the anti-brunette jokes make an explicit comparison with blondes. The following brunette joke list was received via e-mail in April 1997 in Berkeley.

BRUNETTE JOKES!

Being a blonde, I am always, always on the wrong end of the blonde jokes.

Jokes like: What do you call a naked blonde doing a headstand?
A brunette with bad breath.

Well, now it's my turn to get even. Here is a large collection of brunette jokes . . . and some of them are even funny!

Why do brunettes like their dark hair color?
It doesn't show the dirt.

Who makes all the bras for brunettes?
Fisher-Price.

Why didn't Indians scalp brunettes?
They discovered the hair from a buffalo's butt was much more manageable.

Why are brunettes so proud of their hair?
It matches their mustache.

If blondes get fingers run through their hair, what runs through a brunettes hair?
Lice.

How can you tell the color brunette is evil?
You ever see a blonde witch?

Is it true blondes have more fun?
No, they have all the fun.

How can you tell a brunette is lonely?
Check her for a pulse.

What is the most frustrated animal in the world?
A brunette rabbit.

Why did they quit selling Brunette Barbie dolls?
Parents felt the dandruff might be contagious.

Why do brunettes sleep all night on their stomachs?
Because they can.

How do brunettes get the tangles out their hair?
With a rake.

What is the official color of Poland?
Brunette.

How do you drown a brunette fish?
Just add water.

What do you call brunette twins doing bubble gum commercials?
Double-dumb.

What's so good about brunette midgets?
They're only half as ugly.

What would the photograph of a brunette say if it could talk?
Yes.

Why did the brunette chicken cross the road?
Because there were 14,000 roosters on the other side.

What kind of costumes do little brunette kids wear on Halloween?
They don't, they just stand on their heads and go as dirty mops.

Why don't brunettes get breast implants?
They already spent their money on thigh implants.

What did the frustrated brunettes say to her uninterested lover?
"Just what part of the word 'yes' didn't you understand?

Why did God create brunettes?
So ugly men wouldn't be left out.

How can you spot a flock of brunette geese?
They're the ones walking south for the winter.

Where do you find a brunette bat?
Laying dazed on the ground next to the side of the barn.

What do brunettes miss most about a great party?
The invitation.

Where do brunettes get their dark hair?
It's transplanted from their underarms.

What do many brunettes wear on their face that matches their hair?
Warts.

What does a brunette look for all her life and then just dies when she finds one?
A gray hair.

How do you describe a brunette whose phone rings on Saturday night?
Startled.

What do you call a good-looking man with a brunette?
A hostage.

Why did God create brunettes?
Because he screwed up and created the "old maid" category first.

Why do brunettes put ice in their noses before they go to work?
So their lunch won't spoil.

How did Revlon come up with its brunette hair color?
By studying what oil spills did to seaweed.

Why can't a brunette get lost in a crowd of three?
It's easy... if one-third of the crowd is blonde.

What's the mating call of the brunette?
All the blondes are taken!!!

Why are dumb blonde jokes so short?
So brunettes can remember them.

93. Dumb Men Jokes

The blonde jokes, to the extent that they are anti-female have inspired a response in kind. All men, not just blond men, are depicted as being dumb and insensitive. The initial joke in the following two lists of dumb men jokes links the two cycles. The first list was collected from the bulletin board in the Marin General Hospital in Kentfield, California in 1994; the second from Fairfield, Iowa in February 1997. For another version, see FOJ, 54.

DUMB MEN JOKES

WHY ARE ALL DUMB BLOND JOKES ONE-LINERS?
So men can understand them.

WHAT IS THE DIFFERENCE BETWEEN GOVERNMENT BONDS AND MEN?
Government bonds mature.

WHAT'S A MAN'S IDEA OF HELPING WITH THE HOUSEWORK?
Lifting his legs so you can vacuum.

WHAT'S THE DIFFERENCE BETWEEN A MAN AND E.T.?
E.T. phoned home.

WHY IS PSYCHOANALYSIS A LOT QUICKER FOR MEN THAN FOR WOMEN?
When it's time to go back to his childhood, he's already there.

WHAT DID GOD SAY AFTER HE CREATED MAN?
"I can do better than this."

HOW DO MEN DEFINE A "50-50" RELATIONSHIP?
We cook/they eat; we clean/they dirty; we iron/they wrinkle.

WHAT'S THE BEST WAY TO FORCE A MAN TO DO SIT-UPS?
Put the remote control between his toes.

HOW DO MEN EXERCISE AT THE BEACH?
By sucking in their stomachs every time they see a bikini.

WHAT DOES A MAN CONSIDER TO BE A SEVEN-COURSE MEAL?
A hot dog and a six-pack

HOW ARE MEN LIKE NOODLES?
They are always in hot water, they lack taste and they need dough.

WHY IS IT GOOD THAT THERE ARE FEMALE ASTRONAUTS?
When the crew gets lost in space, at least the women will ask for directions.

This is for all you men that loved the dumb blonde jokes.

DUMB MEN JOKES

1. **What is the thinnest book in the world?**
   What men know about women.
2. **How many men does it take to screw in a light bulb?**
   One - men will screw anything.
3. **How does a man take a bubble bath?**
   He eats beans for dinner.
4. **Why do Women rub their eyes when they wake up?**
   Because they don't have balls to scratch.
5. **What's a man's idea of foreplay?**
   A half hour of begging.
6. **How can you tell if a man is sexually excited?**
   He's breathing.
7. **What's the difference between men and government bonds?**
   Bonds mature.
8. **How do you save a man from drowning?**
   Take your foot off his head.
9. **What do men and beer bottles have in common?**
   They both are empty from the neck up.
10. **How can you tell if a man is happy?**
    Who cares.
11. **How many men does it take to change a roll of toilet paper?**
    We don't know - it's never happened.
12. **How are men and parking spots alike?**
    The good ones are always taken and the ones that are left are handicapped.
13. **What's a man's idea of helping with the house work?**
    Lifting his legs so you can vacuum.
14. **What's the difference between a man and E.T.?**
    E.T. phoned home.
15. **What does a man consider a seven course meal?**
    A hot dog and a six pack of beer.

From some of the other lists (not presented here), we find such additional one-liners as:

Husband: Want a quickie? Wife: As opposed to what?

I went to a country fair. They had one of those BELIEVE IT OR NOT shows. They had a man born with a penis and a brain.

Why were men given larger brains than a dog? So they wouldn't hump women's legs at cocktail parties.

How are men like laxatives? They irritate the shit out of you.

Why is it so hard for a woman to find men that are sensitive, caring, and good looking? Because those men already have boyfriends.

94. You Are Now a Woman

The dumb men joke cycle represents an attempt to reverse the stereotype of "smart man/dumb woman." The following joke provides another illustration of that reversal; here we have "dumb man and smart woman." It was collected in Encino, California in April 1995. A second version, which specifically relates the joke to the dumb blonde and dumb men joke cycles, was collected in Berkeley in 1996.

> THREE MEN walking down a beach came across a lamp buried in the sand. They picked it up and began wiping it off. A genie popped out and told them, "I'll grant you each one wish."
> The first man thought to himself, *I have a wonderful wife, a nice car and enough money.* He rubbed the lamp and whispered, "I wish I were ten times smarter."
> "You are now ten times smarter," announced the genie.
> The second guy took the lamp and thought to himself, *I have a wealthy wife and three expensive cars.* So he rubbed the lamp and murmured, "I wish I were a hundred times smarter."
> "You are now a hundred times smarter," the genie mandated.
> The third man thought to himself, *I'm married to an heiress and own a fleet of antique cars.* Then he rubbed the lamp and said, "I wish I were a thousand times smarter."
> The genie pointed at him and declared, "You are now a woman."

There were 3 blondes on a beach . . . one found a bottle, rubbed it, and a genie came out . . . and said he'd grant each one a wish. The first blonde said, "I want to be 25% smarter" . . . poof! He made her a redhead. The second one said, "I want to be 50% smarter" . . . Poof! He made her a brunette. The last one said . . . "but I like this blonde stuff . . . make me 50% dumber"! Poof . . . he made her a man.

95. MENtal Anxiety

The put-down of men continues with the following text collected in Berkeley in mid-1996. It is evidently written from a feminist perspective.

MENtal Anxiety
MENtal Breakdown
MENstrual Cramps
MENopause...

Did you ever notice how all of our problems begin with MEN?

96. He's Shaving You Right Now

One of the acts of stupidity on the part of men, according to women, consists of their making unwelcome sexual advances. The following text from Burlington, Vermont, in April 1994, contains a veiled hint of castration in the female's response to a male pass.

A cute girl was giving a manicure to a man in the barbershop.

The man said, "How about a date later?"

She said, "I'm married."

"So call up your husband and tell him you're going to visit a girlfriend."

She said, "You tell him yourself. He's shaving you right now."

97. Guess What?

Another of the jokes commonly disseminated via the office copier depicts a woman making a fool out of a man. Specifically, a wife surprises her husband. This item is perhaps akin to other "surprise" jokes, e.g., one in which a secretary dupes her boss into disrobing in her apartment, whereupon the entire office staff enters the room singing "Happy Birthday" (cf. WH, 97–99, NLM, 861). In the present case, the joke plays upon a male's fear that he may be observed performing autoerotic acts. The text below was collected from a secretary at the U.S. Steel office in San Francisco in 1969. For other texts of this xerographic joke, see UFFC-TB, 149 (where the term "tallywacker" is used rather than "Jasper"), OG2, 55, and NLM, 861.

There was this business executive that decided he needed a little reprieve from the daily routine so he decided to take his pretty young secretary to a motel and spend the day.

He rented a very nice motel room and they spent the usual day drinking, going to bed, having lunch, drinking some more, going to bed, etc. etc.

Finally five o'clock came and they had to go their separate ways. On the way home, he was thinking about what a nice day it had been and then a horrible thought came to him about what in the world would he tell his wife if she insisted on having a party.

He drove up into the driveway of his home and sure enough there was his wife at the door—she was all arrayed in a pretty gown and negligee, with slippers, pipe and a cool tall drink. She led him into the house with all the sweetness she possessed and to his favorite easy chair.

He thought boy, this is going to lead to something.

They sat back and relaxed sipping on their drinks and talking—suddenly, she stated that she had forgotten something in the bedroom and would be right back.

He thought—oh boy here it comes—when she left he jumped up, unzipped his trousers and pulled 'Jasper' out and started beating and whipping it around, trying to get some life into it—but it did not help a bit. He heard her returning to the room so he stuffed "Jasper" back into his trousers and sat down.

They continued their conversation and then she asked him if he would care for another drink and he replied that he would, so she went off to the kitchen to fix it.

He jumped up and went through the same deal as before but with more vigor—but it did no good. So he just gave up and decided that he would have to tell her that he was just too tired that night.

She returned with their drinks and sat down and said—

"Dear, I have a most wonderful surprise for you and I just know you will be perfectly delighted." He thought—Yes, I guess I will be and said "Well, what is it?"

She said—"Guess what? We're on Candid Camera."

98. Do I Know 'Array 'Awkins?

Perhaps one of the most common complaints about men is that they take their pleasure quickly and totally without regard to women's feelings. The following text consists of a male brag voiced by a victimized woman. The setting and dialect are definitely British, but the text was collected in the Lemont, Pennsylvania in June 1991. Legman presents a parallel text that begins: "Two Cockney girls: 'Do you know 'Arry Brown?' . . . " and indicates that a mimeographed or hektographed version circulated during World War II under the title "Do I know Americans!" (RDJ, 280).

DO I KNOW 'ARRAY 'AWKINS?

Two women met on a London street. One said to the other: "Do you know 'array 'awkins?'

"Do I know 'array 'awkins? Why, it was just the other night when me old man says, Go down and get me a bucket of beer? So I went down and got me a bucket of beer, and who do I meet but 'arry 'awkins. Before I could say 'Trafalgar Square—he grabs me by the ass, shoves me under a tree, downs me, ins me, outs me, wipes his tallywacker on me petticoat, drinks me old man's beer, pisses in the bucket and stalks off whistling, 'God Save the King'—and you ask me do I know 'arry 'awkins?'

99. A Nun Gets on a Bus

Catholicism demands celibacy from priests and nuns, but the folk sometimes question whether vows of chastity are strictly observed. The following joke plays on the disparity between appearance and reality. The first text was collected in Las Vegas in 1994; the second in Berkeley in 1996. For another version, see Alice Kahn and John Dobby Boe, *Your Joke is in the E-Mail: Cyberlaffs from Mousepotatoes* (Berkeley: Ten Speed Press, 1997), 82–83.

A NUN GETS ON A BUS AND SITS BEHIND THE DRIVER, SHE SAYS TO THE BUS DRIVER SHE NEEDS SOMEONE TO TALK TO. SHE LIVES IN A CONVENT AND WANT TO EXPERIENCE SEX BEFORE SHE DIES, THE BUS DRIVER AGREES. THE NUN EXPLAINS SHE CANT HAVE SEX WITH ANYONE WHO IS MARRIED BECAUSE IT WOULD BE A SIN. THE BUS DRIVER SAYS NO PROBLEM, HES NOT MARRIED. THE NUN SAYS SHE ALSO HAS TO DIE A VIRGIN, SO SHE'LL HAVE TO TAKE IT IN THE ASS. THE BUS DRIVER AGREES AGAIN AND BEING THE ONLY PEOPLE ON THE BUS THEY GO TO THE BACK AND TAKE CARE OF BUSINESS. WHEN THEY WERE DONE AND HE HAD RESUMED DRIVING, THE BUS DRIVER SAID "SISTER, I HAVE A CONFESSION TO MAKE, I'M MARRIED AND HAVE THREE KIDS." THE NUN REPLIES THAT'S OK, I HAVE A CONFESSION TOO. MY NAME IS BRUCE AND I'M ON MY WAY TO A "COSTUME PARTY."

This guy is on a bus and sees a nun. He thinks she looks good so he goes up to her and says "Even though you took your vows would you make love to me?" The nun says "NO!" and gets off the bus angrily! The bus driver, who is a guy, says "Excuse me sir, but I couldn't help but overhear your conversation. In case you were wondering, the nun gets off here everyday and goes to pray in Central Park." The other guy says "Thanks, I'm gonna visit her." The next day on the bus the guy is dressed as a priest. He gets off at Central Park and starts praying. Then the nun comes along. When the guy sees her, he says "God has told me to make love to you." They start making out when the priest says "I'm sorry, I haven't been totally honest with you. I'm not really a priest, I'm the guy on the bus yesterday." The nun replies "That's OK, I'm not being totally honest either. I'm really the bus driver!"

100. Three Dogs

Sexuality is considered animalistic by some and for that reason, a number of jokes about sex involve animals. The following joke collected in Berkeley in November 1996 illustrates this tendency.

Three dogs are in the waiting room at the veterinarian's. (A beagle, a great dane and a poodle). The beagle asks the poodle, "Well, I got over the fence, and the neighbor's dog was in heat, and well, I had my way with her, and now I'm here to get fixed." The poodle now asks the beagle: "And what are you in for?" The beagle explains, "Well, my owner had a big party, and a lot of the guests were wearing perfume, and I got kind of excited, and well, I mounted someone's leg... and I'm in here to get fixed, too."

Now the poodle asks the great dane, "What are you here for?" and the great dane tells this story about how his master took a shower and bent over to pick up his towel, and well, he knew it was wrong, but he just couldn't resist...

"So, you're in here to get fixed, too," said the beagle. "Noooo..." said the great dane, "I'm in here to get my nails clipped and something done about my breath."

101. Martians

Sexuality or the theme of human sexual inadequacy can also be projected onto aliens. The following text from Berkeley in July 1996 additionally demonstrates how the "other" is believed to have greater sexual capacity or ability, e.g., this was the case with African Americans and Jews (cf. NLM, 474–83).

MARTIANS

A young man and woman have only been married for two days. One night just as they are getting ready to go to bed, they hear a noise in the backyard, kind of like a vacuum cleaner in reverse. They put on their robes and run outside. There, hovering over the lawn, is a flying saucer.

It lands, and two tall, beautiful, silver aliens get out. Obviously a male and a female, and according to earth standards, quite beautiful. They explain to the newlyweds that they need to stay overnight to effect repairs to their ship.

The young couple agrees, and invites the aliens in for a snack. The aliens agree, but say that it would only be sociable to then invite the newlyweds for a snack. "We will invite you abroad our spacecraft but you must abide by our customs. You must stay the night, and it is only courteous that we change partners for the night." The newlyweds talk it over and agree.

That night, the wife is with the male alien. He undresses and she stares at his perfect body. Then her gaze crosses his groin, and a look of disappointment comes over her. "Is there something wrong?" asks the alien. "Well, you seem so . . . uh . . . small." "No problem," replies the alien, he twists his ear and his organ grows longer. The woman still seems disappointed. She indicates she would like the alien to be "wider." He twists the other ear and grows wider.

The next morning over breakfast, the wife tells her husband what a wonderful night she had with the alien, and that she can hardly wait to share some of the techniques with her husband the next night. "Honey how was your night?" she asks. "Terrible." he said. "The female alien was truly beautiful, but all she did was twist my ears all night long.

102. If the Truth Be Known

Politics may not be as popular a topic for humor as sexuality in the United States, but there are political jokes that are recycled for each new president or generation (cf. WH, 10–11). The following joke was told about Ronald Reagan in the early 1980s. The first text was collected in Downsville, New York, in July 1996, while the second, set in England, was collected in Austin, Texas, at the same time.

IF THE TRUTH BE KNOWN

At a doctors' convention in Switzerland, conversation was taking place in a tavern, after an enthusiastic mid-day lecture.

A Jewish doctor said, "Medicine in my country is so advanced, we can take a kidney out of one person, put it in another, and have him looking for work in six weeks."

A German doctor said, "That's nothing! In Germany, we can take a lung out of one person, put it in another, and have him looking for work in four weeks."

A Russian doctor said, "In my country, medicine is so advanced that we could take half a heart from one person, put it in another, and have both of them looking for work in two weeks."

The American doctor, not to be outdone, said, "Hah! We can take an asshole out of Arkansas, put him in the White House, and half the country will be looking for work the next day!"

After a microsurgeons' conference in New York, the leading surgeons were in the bar and, being drunk as skunks, began to reminisce over their greatest feats.

The first, an Australian surgeon, explained: "We had a chap caught in a printing press at a factory last year and all that was left of him was his little finger. Our team of surgeons constructed a new hand and built a new arm, engineered a new body and ultimately, when he returned to the workforce, he was so efficient, he put 5 men out of work."

"That's nothing," added the American surgeon. "We had a worker trapped inside a nuclear reactor and all that was left of him was his hair. We constructed a new skull, a new torso, and new limbs and returned him to the workforce. He is so efficient now, he has put 50 men out of work."

The English surgeon was not to be outdone: "I was walking down the street when I got the smell of a fart, so I took it back to the hospital in a garbage bag, let it loose on the table, and we got to work. First of all we wrapped an arsehole around it, built a bum around that, attached a body to one end and legs to the other. Gradually it turned into a man called Norman Lamont, and he has put the whole fucking country out of work.

103. How to Make $75,000 a Day

Politicians are not the only authority figures mocked by the folk. Bankers and lawyers are also common targets in humor. The following item has a number of alternative titles, including: "The Chase Manhattan Bank," "The Love of Money," and "Balls." It is basically a trickster tale with the unusual feature of having a little old lady as the trickster figure. The text was collected in Iselin, New Jersey in July 1995.

This joke is an extremely popular one. It appeared in the important 1928 collection *Anecdota Americana*. See the reprint edition, *The Classic Book of Dirty Jokes* (New York: Bell, 1981), 144. For a similar version, see "Mr. J," *Giant Book of Dirty Jokes* (New York: Castle, 1984), 32–33. In these versions, a boy with a gambling problem bets fifty cents with his female teacher that she is having her period. She shows him that she is not, but when she reports to the boy's father that she believes she has cured the boy's gambling habit, the father confesses that the boy bet him five dollars that he would see the teacher's private parts that very day. For other versions of this joke, see RDJ, 107–08, NLM, 178–79, 543–44, and FOJ, 262. For a Romanian version with a political slant, see C. Banc and A. Dundes, *First Prize: Fifteen Years! An Annotated Collection of Romanian Political Jokes* (Cranbury, New Jersey: Associated Univ. Presses, 1986), 148–49. For a discussion of eight versions of this joke, see Linda Dégh, "The Bet," in Christoph Schmitt, ed. *Homo narrans* (Münster: Waxman, 1999) pp. 191–200.

HOW TO MAKE $75,000 A DAY

A little old lady walked into the main branch of Chase Manhattan Bank with a large paper bag in her hand. She told the young teller at the window that she wished to take the 3 million dollars in her bag and open an account. First, she said, "I want to meet the president of Chase Manhattan because of the large amount of money involved." The teller seemed to think this was a reasonable request, after opening the paper bag and seeing bundles of $1000 bills. He telephoned the bank president's secretary to obtain an appointment for the lady.

The little old lady was escorted upstairs into the president's office. Introductions were made and she stated that she wanted to know the people she did business with on a personal level. The bank president then asked her how she came into such a large amount of money "Was it an inheritance?" he asked. "No," she replied. He was quiet for a minute, trying to think where this little old lady could possible have come into $3 million. . . . "I bet," she stated.

"YOU BET!" repeated the bank president, "As in horses?" "No," she replied, "I bet on people." Seeing his confusion she explained that she just bet different things with people. Suddenly she said, "I'll bet you 25,000 dollars that by 10:00 tomorrow morning, your balls will be square." The bank president figured that she must be off her rocker and decided to accept her bet. He didn't see how he could lose. For the rest of the day, he was very careful. He decided to stay home that evening and take no chances and retire early—there was $25,000 at stake.

After he awoke and took his shower, he carefully checked to assure everything was OK. There was no change, he looked the same as always. He went to work and waited for the little old lady to come in at 10:00 humming as he went. He knew it would be a good day, how often do you get $25,000 for doing nothing? At 10:00 sharp, the little old lady was shown into his office, with her a younger man. When he inquired as to the man's purpose for being there she informed him he was her lawyer and that she took him along whenever money was involved. "Well," she asked, "what about our bet?" "I don't know how to tell you," he replied, "But I'm the same as always, only $25,000 richer." The lady seemed to accept this, but requested that she see for herself. The bank president thought that this was reasonable and dropped his trousers. She instructed him to bend over and then she grabbed his testicles. Sure enough, everything was fine. The bank president then jumped up and saw the lawyer standing across the room violently banging his head against the wall, "What's wrong with him?" the banker inquired. "Oh him," she replied. "I bet him $100,000 that by 10:00 this morning I'd have the president of the Chase Manhattan Bank by the balls!!"

104. I Cut, I Cut

The Chase-Manhattan Bank seems to be a popular venue for photocopier jokes. Increased trade with Asian nations has influenced American banks which seek contacts with flourishing Asian businesses. At the same time, there is some popular sentiment to the effect that the United States is being inundated with Asian products, e.g., Japanese cars, television sets, etc. There is an impression that some Asian business concerns are so competitive that they will cut export prices drastically in order to make a sale. It is possible that the reference to cutting in the last line of the following joke may reflect the American perception of such a policy. The text was collected in the Capay Valley, California, in February 1997. For a Russian version told about Georgians, see Emil A. Draitser, *Taking Penguins to the Movies: Russian Ethnic Humor* (Detroit: Wayne State Univ. Press, 1998), 51. For an earlier version accompanied by the comment that it was told "only by women," see NLM, 466.

The president of Chase Manhattan Bank decides he should take a vacation/business trip. Since the president has heard about how fun Taipei is, he decides to visit the offices there. He books two tickets, one for him and one for his secretary.

After his arrival in Taipei, the president receives an urgent message from headquarters that the richest man in Taiwan wants to put all his money into a Chase Manhattan account. Since the account would be quite substantial, the president decides to meet personally with the man.

The next day, the president and his secretary go to meet the Taiwanese businessman at a really expensive restaurant. Throughout the dinner, the president tries to bring up the subject of opening the account for the Taiwanese businessman. However, the prospective client only seems to be interested in the president's secretary.

After dinner, the businessman asks the secretary to spend the rest of the evening seeing the sights in Taipei with him. Not wishing to offend the prospective client, the president orders his secretary to spend some time with the man. He tells her that she must be diplomatic and under no circumstances is she to insult the man by rejecting him outright.

After going to a dance club for a few hours, the businessman takes the secretary aside. As he holds her hand and looks her straight in the eyes, he tells her that he loves her. Then, he gets on his knees and asks her to marry him.

Naturally, the secretary is quite taken aback. However, she remembers what her boss told her. Don't reject the guy outright. So, she tries to think of a way to dissuade the businessman from wanting to marry her. So, after a few minutes, the woman says to the man, "I will only marry you under three conditions. First, I want my engagement ring to be a 75 carat diamond ring, with a matching 200 carat diamond tiara."

The Taiwanese man pauses for awhile. Then, he nods his head and says, "No problem!! I buy. I buy."

Realizing that her first condition was too easy, the woman says to the man, "I want you to build me a 100 room mansion in New York. As a vacation home, I want a chateau built in the middle of the best wine country in France."

The man pauses for awhile. He whips out his cellular phone, calls some brokers in New York, then he calls some brokers in France. He looks at the woman, nods his head and says, "Okay, okay. I build, I build."

Realizing that she has one last condition, the secretary knows that she'd better make this a good one. She takes her time to think and finally, she gets an idea. A sure-to-work condition. She squints her eyes, looks at the man and says, rather coldly, "Since I like to have sex, I want the man I marry to have a 12-inch penis."

The man seems a bit disturbed. He cups his face with his hands and rests his elbows on the table. All the while, he's muttering something in Chinese. Finally, after what seemed like forever, the man shakes his head, looking real sad, says to the woman, "I cut. I cut."

105. The Old Miser

In lawyer jokes, the lawyer is usually depicted as unscrupulous, greedy, and clever. The following classic text, also popular in oral tradition, was collected in Burlington, Vermont in April 1994. It is often found in anthologies of lawyer jokes. For typical texts, see Larry Wilde, *The Official Lawyers Joke Book* (New York: Bantam, 1982), 162; and Blanche Knott, *Truly Tasteless Lawyer Jokes* (New York: St. Martin's, 1990), 70.

As the old miser lay in bed dying, he called his doctor, lawyer, and minister to his bedside. " I have always heard you can't take it with you but I'm going to prove you can." said the old man. "I have $90,000 in three envelopes under my mattress. I want each of you to take one and as they throw the dirt on me I want you to toss the envelopes in."

On the way back from the cemetery the minister said, "I feel guilty. I needed $10,000 for the building fund and only threw $20,000 in the grave." The doctor said, "I, too must confess: I am building a new wing on the hospital, needed $20,000 and only threw in $10,000." The lawyer said "Gentlemen, I'm shocked and ashamed of you. At least I have some integrity. I threw in my personal check for the full amount."

106. I Will Grant You Three Wishes

Lawyers have become such a popular scapegoat for American society's ills that standard folktales have been adapted to target them. The following item was reported in San Francisco in December 1996, and the unwary reader might assume that it is a joke of recent origin, especially in view of the explicit reference to organ transplants. However, folklore is like a chameleon in its extraordinary capacity to be updated and localized to fit an infinite variety of diverse scenarios. In this case, the text is easily identifiable as an ancient Indo-European tale type, namely, Aarne-Thompson 1331, The Covetous and the Envious. The summary reads: "Of two envious men, one is given the power of fulfilling any wish, on condition that the other shall receive double. He wishes that he may lose an eye."

The tale is considered to be in the Aesopic tradition. Specifically, it is fable 22 in the collection of forty-two compiled by Avianus in the early fifth century. The tale includes motif J 2074, Twice the Wish to the Enemy. For the Latin text, see Avianus, *Oeuvres,* ed. Leon Herrmann, Collection Latomus, XCVI (Bruxelles: Latomus, 1968), 46. For an English rendering, see Ben Edwin Perry, ed., *Babrius and Phaedrus* (Cambridge: Harvard Univ. Press, 1975), 532–33. For a modern poetic translation titled "The Greedy and the Envious Man," see *The Fables* of *Avianus* (Baltimore: Johns Hopkins Univ. Press, 1993), 30. German folklorist Kurt Ranke, in the entry on Avianus in the *Enzyklopädie des Märchens,* even remarks on this tale's popularity inasmuch as it is to be found in modern collections of jokes. See *Enzyklopädie des Märchens,* 1(4) (1976), 1104. Legman reports a version from New York City in 1936: "A Jew in heaven is told that whatever he asks for, Hitler will get double. He asks that one of his testicles be removed." (See NLM, 611). In that context it is noteworthy that in the version presented here, the consequences are more serious in terms of the loss of the body organs in question.

The exceptional span of this item's life in tradition—over the course of more than fifteen hundred years—is a marvelous testament to the staying power of folklore through time and space. The tale is found from India to Spain, as well as in the New World. We present a second version of the same tale, collected in Berkeley in November of 1999, which involves a different organ.

Did you hear about the guy on the beach who found a bottle? He rubbed it and, sure enough, out popped a Genie.

"I will grant you three wishes," replied the Genie. "But there's a catch.

"The man was ecstatic. "What catch?" he asked.
The Genie replied, "Every time you make a wish, every lawyer in the world will receive DOUBLE what you asked for."
"Well, I can live with that! No problem!" replied the elated man.
"What is your first wish?" asked the Genie.
"Well, I've always wanted a Ferrari!"
POOF! A Ferrari appeared in front of the man.
"NOW, every lawyer in the world has TWO Ferrari's," said the Genie. "Next wish?"
"I'd LOVE a million dollars . . . " replied the man. POOF! One million dollars appeared at his feet.
"NOW, every lawyer in the world has TWO MILLION dollars," said the Genie.
"Well, that's okay, as long as I've got MY million," replied the man. "What is your final wish?"
The man thought long and hard, and finally said, "Well, you know, I've always wanted to donate a kidney. . . ."

Subject: women are bad!!

Three women were out golfing one day and one of them hit her ball into the woods. She went into the woods to look for it and found a frog in a trap.

The frog said to her, "If you release me from this trap, I will grant you 3 wishes." The woman freed the frog and the frog said, "Thank you, but I failed to mention that there was a condition to your wishes - that whatever you wish for, your husband will get 10 times more or better!" The woman said, "That would be okay,"

For her first wish, she wanted to be the most beautiful woman in the world. The frog warned her, "You do realize that this wish will also make your husband the most handsome man in the world, an Adonis, that women will flock to."

The woman replied, "That will be okay because I will be the most beautiful woman and he will only have eyes for me." So, POOF - she's the most beautiful woman in the world!

For her second wish, she wanted to be the richest woman in the world. The frog said, "That will make your husband the richest man in the world and he will be ten times richer than you." The woman said, "That will be okay because what is mine is his and what is his is mine." So, POOF - she's the richest woman in the world!

The frog then inquired about her third wish, and she answered, "I'd like a mild heart attack."

Moral of the story: Women are bad . . . .

107. Kingsview Mental Hospital

Another common theme of contemporary humor involves psychiatrists and mental patients. The following text from Burlington, Vermont, collected in April 1994, is a case in point. For another version, see Karen Warner, *500 Great Bartender's Jokes* (New York: Penguin, 1993), 83–84, in which version a "manhole cover" appears in the punchline.

When a busload of people entered a large restaurant, the leader of the group approached the manager.

"Sir, I'm Mr. Phillips of the Kingsview Mental Hospital. These nice folks are mental patients in our halfway house program. They've all been cured, but they do have one small problem: They will want to pay you in bottle caps. So if you'll be so kind as to humor them in this way, I'll take care of the bill when they are through."

The manager, wanting to be a good citizen, collected the bottle caps. The leader returned and with gratitude said, Thank you so very much. I'll pay the bill now. Do you have change for a hubcap?"

108. Parrot Boss

The parrot has long been a familiar character in oral humor, probably because of its apparent ability to imitate human speech. It is not surprising, therefore, that several parrot jokes have entered the stream of photocopier tradition as well. (For a discussion of parrot jokes, see RDJ, 199–206.) The following text was collected in Santa Clara, California in 1996.

A MAN GOES to a pet shop to buy a parrot. "We have three," says the clerk. "This blue one speaks four languages and costs $1000, and the red parrot knows six languages and costs $2000. The orange one over there costs $3000, but doesn't talk at all."

"Three thousand!" exclaims the man. "How come so much?"

"Well," the clerk goes on, "we don't know what he does, but the other two call him 'boss.'"

109. A Short Day

The parrot as observer and commentator on human events is well demonstrated in the following text reported in the San Francisco Bay Area in the 1940s. It has been collected coast to coast since that time. (For a New York City version from 1953, see RDJ, 203; for another version from the same period, see J. M. Elgart, *Over Sexteen* (New York: Elgart Publishing Co. 1951), 24.

> She woke up in the morning, put on her robe, went downstairs, raised the blind, took the cover off the parrot, went to the kitchen, put the coffee on, and lit the fire.
>
> The telephone rang, and her boy friend said, "Hi-ya, Babe, I just got off the ship, fix yourself up, I'm coming right over." She hung up the telephone, pulled down the blind, took off the coffee, and turned off the fire. She then came back in the living room and put the cover back on the parrot, and began slipping off her robe. As she started up the stairs, the parrot called out after her, "Kee-Rist, this sure has been a short day".

110. Jesus Is Watching You

Another parrot joke concerns the anxiety of homeowners and others with respect to a common fear of burglary. Protective measures run the gamut from electronic alarm and surveillance systems to the old fashioned watchdog. The first version of the following item was collected in Berkeley, California in June 1997. The second version was also collected in Berkeley in December of 1998. For another photocopier item referring to a similar home security theme, see NT, 122–23.

Late one night, a burglar broke into a house he thought was empty.

He tiptoed through the living room but suddenly he froze in his tracks when he heard a loud voice say, "Jesus is watching you!"

Silence returned to the house, so the burglar crept forward again.

The burglar stopped dead again. He was frightened. Frantically, he looked all around. In a dark corner, he spotted a bird cage and in the cage was a parrot.

He asked the parrot: "Was that you who said Jesus is watching me?"

"Yes" said the parrot.

The burglar breathed a sigh of relief, and asked the parrot: "What's your name?"

"Clarence," said the bird.

"That's a dumb name for a parrot," sneered the burglar. "What idiot named you Clarence?"

The parrot replied: "The same idiot who named the Rottweiller Jesus."

```
> Keeping an Eye on Things
>
> A burglar broke into a house one night. He shined his flashlight around,
> looking for valuables, and when he picked up a CD player to place in his
> sack, a strange, disembodied voice echoed from the dark saying, "Jesus is
> watching you."
>
>    He nearly jumped out of his skin, clicked his flashlight off and froze.
> When he heard nothing more, after a bit he shook his head, promised
> himself a vacation after the next big score, then clicked the light back
> on and began searching for more valuables. Just as he pulled the stereo
> out so he could disconnect the wires, clear as a bell he heard, "Jesus is
> watching you."
>
>    Freaked out, he shined his light around frantically, looking for the
> source of the voice. Finally, in the corner of the room, his flashlight
> beam came to rest on a parrot. "Did you say that?" He hissed at the
> parrot. "Yep," the parrot confessed, then squawked, "I am just trying to
> warn you." The burglar relaxed.
>
> "Warn me huh? Who the hell are you?" "Moses," replied the bird. "Moses?"
> the burglar laughed. "What kind of stupid people would name a parrot
> Moses?"
>
>    The bird promptly answered, "Probably the same kind of people that
> would name a Rotweiller Jesus..."
>
```

111. A Commuter on the London Underground

The generation gap may produce hostility and a lack of understanding. The following text, set in England, but collected in Iselin, New Jersey, in July 1995, illustrates this. For another version, see Alice Kahn and John Dobby Boe, *Your Jokes Is in the E-Mail: Cyberlaffs from Mousepotatoes* (Berkeley: Ten Speed Press, 1997), 92.

A commuter on the London Underground was sitting minding his own business and quietly watching a punk rocker sitting opposite him who had an orange Mohican cut down the middle of his head with yellow hair on one side and blue hair on the other side. He was listening to his personal stereo and writhing to the rhythm in his seat.

The punk caught the commuter staring at him and in a loud East London accent said, "What do you fink yor staring at?" The commuter replied that he was more than a little fascinated by his appearance, to which the punk responded, "Ain't you ever done nuffink radical in your life then, eh?"

The commuter said, "Well, as a matter of fact, about seventeen years ago I fucked a parrot and I was wondering if you were my son!"

112. Lion Tamer Audition

It could be argued that the underlying rationale of zoos and circus acts is the pleasure in seeing wild animals, representing the animal nature of man (the id) caged or controlled, but yet with the possibility, albeit slim, of these animals escaping, overwhelming or attacking their human captors. In this symbolic nature-culture opposition, culture or civilization does not always prevail, and raw animality may be unleashed. This theme is, we believe, manifested in the following two texts, the first from Mountain View, California, in 1991, the second from Loveland, Colorado in 1992.

At the circus the lion tamer gets sick and a replacement must be found before the next show, so a call does out to the entertainment community looking for another animal trainer. Two people respond for the job, a man and a woman.

When they arrive for an audition, the circus manager sends the woman in the cage first and to see if she's got the right stuff, he sends out the biggest and meanest lion in his menagerie. The lion seems to be in no mood to be tamed this day and endlessly circles the woman getting more threatening at every pass. He knocks the chair out of her hand with a swipe of his paw. The next swipe dispatches her whip. A third swipe knocks the gun out of her hand leaving her completely defenseless.

As the lion closes in for the kill, the woman rips open her blouse, displaying a bodacious set of knockers. The lion stops dead in his tracks and lies down as she allows him to cuddle and lick her tits.

The circus manager then turns to the male waiting for his audition and asks, "Do you so suppose you can do as well as that?" He replies, "Bet yer ass, but first get that damn lion outta there."

There is this little wussy guy and he's sitting at a bar. We'll call him Jordan and he's sitting there and it's kinda a crazy bar and everyone is kinda big and manly and at the end of the bar was this alligator.

Well he thought there was some pretty big manly guys in there when all of a sudden this huge guy walks through the door, we'll call him Jim. He's really big and huge and buff. And he walks over to the end of the table, right where the alligator is. He walks up to the alligator and goes "Pow" (Jim hits fist down on table). Hits the alligator right between the eyes. The alligator opens his mouth and the guy walks up to him and kinda unzips his pants and whips out his dick and sticks it in the alligator's mouth. Hits it again really hard right between the eyes "Pow." The alligator closes its mouth. The guy sits there 5-10 minutes. Really starts to enjoy himself and right after he's finished he reaches down and hits the alligator again. The alligator opens his mouth. The guy turns around, obviously finished, and zips his pants back up. He looks out to the bar and he says "I will give anyone $500 if they will do that."

And little Jordan raises his hand and says, "Okay, okay, I'll do it. But you got to promise not to hit me so hard."

Offbeat Beasthood

Animals have provided an important source of metaphors for nearly all aspects of the human condition. Common American folk similes and folk metaphors include: "birdbrain," "cat's paw," "lame duck," "dog-tired," "stubborn as a mule," "snake in the grass," "rat race," "as wise as an owl," and many, many others. (For many more illustrations, see Joseph D. Clark, *Beastly Folklore* (Metuchen, New Jersey: Scarecrow Press, 1968); and Robert A. Palmatier, *Speaking of Animals: A Dictionary of Animal Metaphors* (Westport, Conn.: Greenwood Press, 1995). Photocopier tradition is exemplified by such phrases as "When You're Up To Your Ass In Alligators," and "Never Try To Teach a Pig To Sing." Man's relationship to animals ranges from owning pets to hunting wild game. The following chapter presents a representative sampling of animal imagery in xerographic folklore.

113. Pick the Winning Racehorse!

Human interest in animals includes their role in sporting events. From bull fights, cockfights, and dogfights to sheep herding trials and horse and dog racing, animals provide a source of entertainment. Even the naming of athletic teams reflects a definite penchant for animal totems or symbols, e.g., California Golden Bears, UCLA Bruins, Washington Huskies, Arizona Wildcats. Professional teams also frequently employ animal names and mascots, e.g., the Chicago Bears, the Philadelphia Eagles, or the Miami Dolphins.

Horse racing is an ancient sport and, like so many such pastimes, involves betting. The object is to place one's bet before the race on the horse destined to win. The following cartoon presents an obvious choice to the viewer. It was collected in Denton, Texas in 1991. The pseudo-test format of the item is reminiscent of other photocopier puzzles (cf. "Is This Test Too Tough?" in NT, 246–51).

Pick the Winning Racehorse!

Which of these two racehorses will win the race?

Answer here A ☐ or B ☐

114. Whoa!

Horses have long been a critical mode of transportation. This has necessitated the development of techniques to train such animals. The tension between the animal's normal independent spirit and the rider's need to control the horse's energy and strength is a constant factor in both horse racing and the use of the horse as a means of locomotion. The image of a horse going "over the edge" of a precipice is meant to illustrate a frustrating situation in which the rider finds himself in jeopardy after having lost control of his mount. The following item was collected in 1980 in Winnipeg, Canada.

There is an oral tale that involves a similar theme. A preacher buys a horse from a horse trader who advises him that the horse is extremely fast and has been trained in a special way. It responds to just two commands: "Thank God" to make it go; "Amen" to make it stop. The preacher says he understands and gets on the horse. He says, "Thank God," and the horse takes off like the wind. He's never had such a ride in his life. Suddenly he sees that there's a steep cliff two hundred yards dead ahead. In a panic, he tries to remember the command to stop the horse. "Whoa," he says, but to no avail. "Stop," "Halt," but nothing works. Realizing that he's facing his doom, he quickly recites the "Lord's Prayer" ending with "Amen." The horse responds immediately screeching to a stop right at the edge of the precipice. The preacher mops his brow, lifts his eyes heavenward, and says "Thank God!"

115. Attitude

An animal that refuses to obey its master's commands might be said in modern parlance, to have an "attitude." The term implies a belligerent, surly, antisocial stance. It may well have originated in African-American folk speech in the early 1970s, but it has become a part of the everyday, general American lexicon, as the following item, collected in Encino, California, in April 1995, attests. The use of a wolf, which in European-American folklore is the archetypal villain, makes the image especially forceful. It should be noted that the wolf has borrowed the well-known human gesture of defiance, namely the *digitus impudicus*. For references to this gesture, see #84 above; for discussions of "attitude," see Frederic G. Cassidy, ed., *Dictionary of American Regional English*, Vol. I (Cambridge: Harvard Univ. Press, 1985), 104, and also Clarence Major, ed., *Juba to Jive: A Dictionary of African-American Slang* (New York: Viking, 1994), 104. For another version of this item, see OH2, 88.

116. It's Been a Great Year!

The versatility of the wolf is demonstrated in the following item collected in Chicago in 1994. Here the wolf is not at all aggressive, but rather, is on the verge of starvation (as indicated by the condition of its ribs) and is in generally wretched shape, with its tail between its legs, a common metaphor for retreat or defeat. The caption is obviously a tongue-in-cheek commentary on a disastrous economic season. For another version, see UOH, 76.

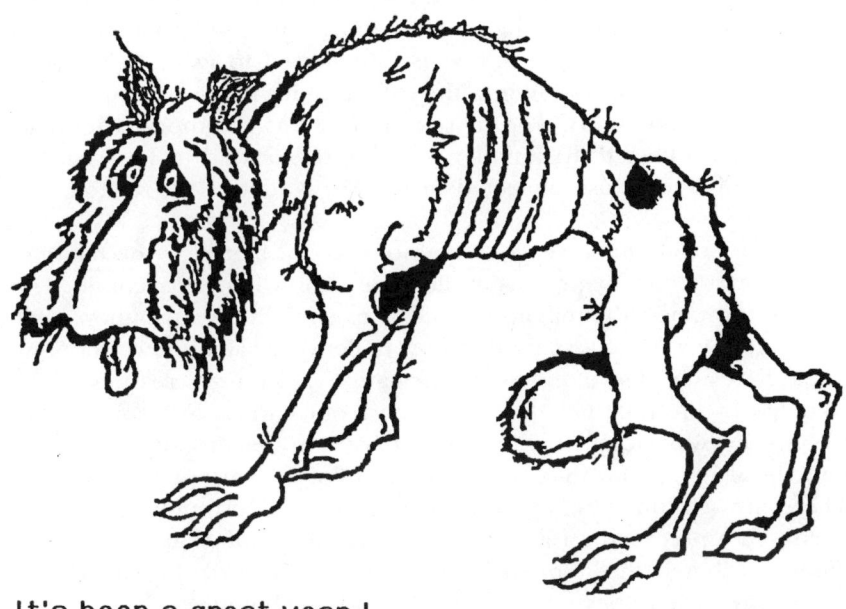

It's been a great year !

117. How to Housebreak Your Dog

The following folk cartoon borrows from comic strip technique to present a series of drawings. The problem of housebreaking or curbing a pet dog is one faced by most dog owners. Some owners tend to treat their pets as human beings, e.g., by dressing them in "human" clothing, by feeding them human foods, leaving them at doggy hotels, paying for top medical care, and finally burying them in cemeteries with full ritual (often, in addition, naming them as beneficiaries in their will). It seems clear that dogs and cats may serve as surrogate children for childless adults. Dogs that are treated as little humans are asked to observe toilet training rituals, e.g., urinating or defecating at a particular time of day or at a particular location. A dog is thus forced to learn to adapt to human culture by responding to the calling of his name and by controlling his waste functions. The first version of this common cartoon sequence was collected in Berkeley in 1970, the second in Las Vegas in 1994. A third text, also collected in Las Vegas in 1994, is related only by theme.

Among our multiple versions, we note several that bear the name of famous cartoonist Ernie Bushmiller, best known for his comic strip "Nancy." However, the majority of our texts contain no attribution whatsoever. If one were to assume that Bushmiller originated the cartoon, we would have an instance of how a professional cartoonist's creation can be co-opted by the folk. On the other hand, our earliest text comes from ISR in 1964 with no attribution. At that point in time, it was much more difficult, if not impossible, to publish scatological cartoons of this sort. There are a number of alternative possibilites: Bushmiller may have borrowed a preexisting folklore item, or an anonymous artist may have falsely attributed the item to Bushmiller. The style of the cartoon sequence, however, does resemble his drawing technique.

The second version has sixteen, rather than six, sections and seems to have been drawn in a completely different style. For a version reported in Sweden, see MF, 51; for a version in England, see RIF, 75.

I've spoken before about my very inventive neighbor and his wife. A lovely couple that recently got a new puppy. The worst time to try to housebreak a dog is in cold weather. During the recent freeze, he would bundle himself up and take the dog out on the grass.

Well, the dog hated it more than my neighbor. The pooch's feet would freeze right up and he'd go yelping back to the house. The trainer tried everything. Nothing worked — until he got a bright idea.

He went to the drug store and bought a pack of 12 condoms. Now he's past the point of "foolin' around," so the girl behind the counter gave him a funny look while ringing it up. He felt a little squirmish, but returned home with his experiment.

He put one on each of the dog's paws and sent him out the front door. It made for a funny sight to see the animal running around the lawn with these things on. And — he tore them to shreds. It didn't work.

My neighbor's wife suggested: "Maybe you need to try a stronger brand!"

He went back to the store to the same cashier and said, "I need 12 more of these in a stronger brand." The girl became wide-eyed and said, "Well, all right!"

My neighbor felt uneasy and mumbled, "They're not for me. They're for my dog."

It's nice to have nutty neighbors.

118. Lonely at the Top

In many businesses and other organizations, there is a strict hierarchical structure. A mountain or pyramid may serve to illustrate the hierarchy such that the higher up one goes, the smaller the space. In theory, the individual at the very top of the pyramid is alone, perhaps without peers or friends. This has given rise to the idea that it may be "lonely at the top." In addition, the power that accrues to the top dog may be misused or abused such that underlings may have to endure unwelcome duties. The following cartoon collected in Eureka, California, in November 1989, depicts the latter situation. For other photocopier renderings of organizational hierarchy, with its attendant disagreeable features, see WH, 163–65, SD 13–15.

119. Louisiana Mosquito

There is no limit to the animals that can be selected by the folk imagination for portrayal. The following item collected in Kokomo, Indiana, in 1976, displays a superphallic mosquito, and reveals a form of exaggeration normally attributed to Texas. The cross-species intercourse may or may not be an allusion to attitudes and laws against miscegenation.

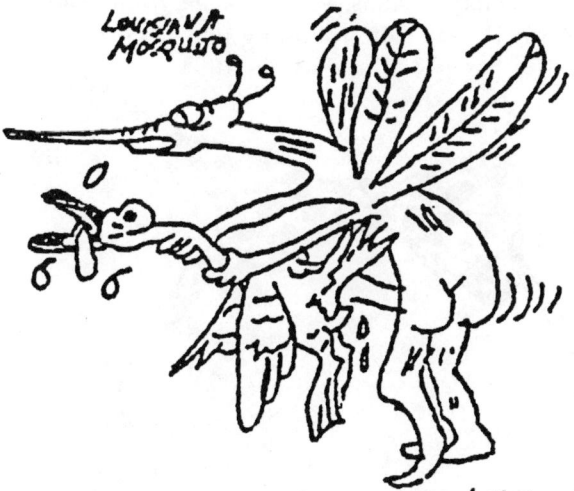

120. How Easter Eggs Are Made!!!

The two animals most closely associated with Easter are the Easter Bunny and the provider of eggs, namely, the hen. The fact that the Easter Bunny, a male, is nominally credited with bringing eggs, which were normally produced by a *female* chicken, suggests a decidedly male bias in this ritual occasion. See Alan Dundes, "The Crowing Hen and the Easter Bunny: Male Chauvinism in American Folklore," in Linda Dégh, Henry Glassie, and Felix J. Oinas, eds., *Folklore Today* (Bloomington: Indiana Univ., 1976), 123–38. The following item, in greeting card format, was collected in Savage, Minnesota in 1994.

HAPPY EASTER!

121. As Much as I Can Stand

Sexuality may not always be unalloyed pleasure. There may be a price to pay, either literally or figuratively. Gigolos or prostitutes, performing for pay, may have to endure unpleasant experiences. The following item, collected in Bloomington, Indiana, in 1976, has an implicit (rather than explicit) reference to cross-species intercourse. Presumably, the dog has to suffer the strong smell of the skunk during his carnal activity.

122. Gathering Nuts

The following item is yet another instance of an interspecies encounter. In this case, there is a play on the slang term "nuts" (meaning testicles). The small squirrel is able to paralyze the larger bear by holding him by his scrotum. The quizzical expression on the bear's face may reflect either surprise or fear (of the nut-eating squirrel with its protruding castratory teeth), or both. There is an idiom in American folk speech, "to have someone by the balls," meaning to have someone under complete control. For a discussion of this idiom, known to men since World War II, see Harold Wentworth and Stuart Berg Flexner, *Dictionary of American Slang* (New York: Thomas Y. Crowell, 1967), 17. The first version was collected in Kokomo, Indiana (see also item 103 above) in 1976; the second from Menlo Park, California in 1991.

224   *Why Don't Sheep Shrink When It Rains?*

123. Mouse Balls

The computer has become a factor in American folklore as numerous photocopier items attest (cf. SD 6–7, NT 161–67, WY, 203–04). One of the common components of computers is a hand-held control device that manipulates a cursor, e.g., an "arrow" on the computer screen, this cursor being utilized to select among various options.

This device is known as a "mouse" perhaps because its shape is somewhat similar to the body of that particular rodent. With such a name, it was only a question of time before the folk seized upon the term for purposes of humor. Inside the base of the mouse is a spherical "ball," which rotates on a flat surface (a desk pad), and it is this ball that designates the desired movement of the cursor on the screen. The following item, which has been reported from a variety of geographical locations in the United States, was collected in Berkeley in 1995.

This is an actual alert to the IBM Field Engineers that went out to all IBM Branch Offices.

Abstract: Mouse Balls available as FRU (Field Replacement Units)

Mouse balls are now available as FRU. Therefore, if a mouse fails to operate or should it perform erratically, it may need a ball replacement. Because of the delicate nature of this procedure, replacement of mouse balls should only be attempted by properly trained personnel.

Before proceeding, determine the type of mouse balls by examining the underside of the mouse. Domestic balls will be larger and harder than foreign balls. Ball removal procedures differ depending upon manufacturer of the mouse. Foreign balls can be replaced by using the pop-off method. Domestic balls are replaced using the twist-off method. Mouse balls are not usually static sensitive. However, excessive handling can result in sudden discharge. Upon completion of ball replacement, the mouse may be used immediately.

It is recommended that each replacer have a pair of spare balls for maintaining optimum customer satisfaction, and that any customer missing his balls should suspect local personnel of removing these necessary items.

To reorder, specify on the following:
P/N 33F8462 - Domestic Mouse Balls
P/N 33F8461 - Foreign Balls

(January 10, 1995)

124. Computer Mouse

In folk fantasy, one can imagine that the "mouse" resents being pushed around endlessly by a giant human hand. Accordingly, a large mouse takes revenge by means of a dramatic reversal, such that it can manipulate with its paw a miniaturized human who must remain passive and compliant. The first version was collected from a legal secretary in San Francisco in December 1995; the second in Edmonds, Washington in November 1996. Despite its probable creation in 1995 or so, there is considerable variation that has occurred in a relatively short amount of time, variation in the mouse's tail, fingers, nose, and eye, as well as in the computer screen and the miniature human figure.

125. She Was a Tough One

In American folklore, the farmer and the farm provide a convenient locus for sexual adventures. Jokes concerning the traveling salesman and the farmer's daughter are classic Americana. See Erika K. Clowes, "Oedipal Themes in Latency: Analysis of the 'Farmer's Daughter' Joke," *The Psychoanalytic Study of the Child*, 51 (1996), 436–54.

The apparent innocence or naiveté of women is a common theme in male-centered fantasies. In the following traditional item, a scantily dressed female in high-heeled shoes, totally inappropriate attire for working on a farm, is depicted as having mistakenly milked a bull instead of a cow. The manipulation of the bull's pizzle has evidently given the animal pleasure, but has at the same time exhausted and unnerved the beast. In the first version of this item, collected at an Air Force base near Sacramento in 1978, the bull's organ is given human characteristics and is explicitly depicted. This is in contrast to the second version from Las Vegas, Nevada in June 1994. Other variation occurs with respect to the background, the dress and the figure of the farmer, the legs on the milking stool, and even the hooves of the bull and the presence or absence of a ring in the bull's nose.

The suggested equivalence of male semen and a milk product, e.g., cream (as in the expression "cream one's jeans," meaning to ejaculate in one's pants) is probably implicit in this traditional cartoon.

"She was a tough one — but I finally got a bucket full!"

126. What are You Laughing At?

Another illustration of the milking maneuver is provided by a very traditional, widely diffused classic cartoon that has been in continuous circulation since the mid-1940s. In this item, the naive female milks a cow, not a bull, but a crafty male places his organ near the cow's udder with predictable results. We shall present a number of versions to demonstrate the item's remarkable stability and variation. The first version is from ISR and is dated 1947. The second version was collected in San Francisco in 1979; the third from Downsville, New York in July 1996; the fourth from Savage, Minnesota in August 1994; the fifth version, in greeting card format, was collected in Oakland, California in August 1976; while the sixth, and last, version was collected in Wilmington, Delaware in 1991.

"WHAT THE HELL ARE YOU GRINNING AT?"

"Thank God I'm a Country Boy"!!

MILKING TIME ON THE FARM

127. What Happens from Drinking Too Much Milk

The symbolic equation of male phallus and cow's teat, which will no doubt surprise some readers, cannot be gainsaid in the light of the following cartoon, which sometimes occurs in greeting card format with the caption on the front, followed by the image on the second page. The previous items depicted milking a phallus, whereas this item suggests that the consumption of milk produces a cow-like penile udder. (For other texts involving the comparison of a cow's teat to a man's penis, see NLM, 601). The confusion of phallus and breast, as illustrated in this cartoon, might be construed as intimating that men may suffer from what could be termed "breast envy."

The first version was collected in Burlington, Vermont in April 1994; the second from Downsville, New York in July 1996; while the third, a German version, was collected in Göttingen in May 1988. Appropriately enough, the German version includes an encomium for beer: "This is what happens if a person drinks only milk instead of beer." We might note that there are oral texts referring to multiple phalluses, e.g., "Did you hear about the guy with 5 peckers? He had tailor-made shorts that fit like a glove."

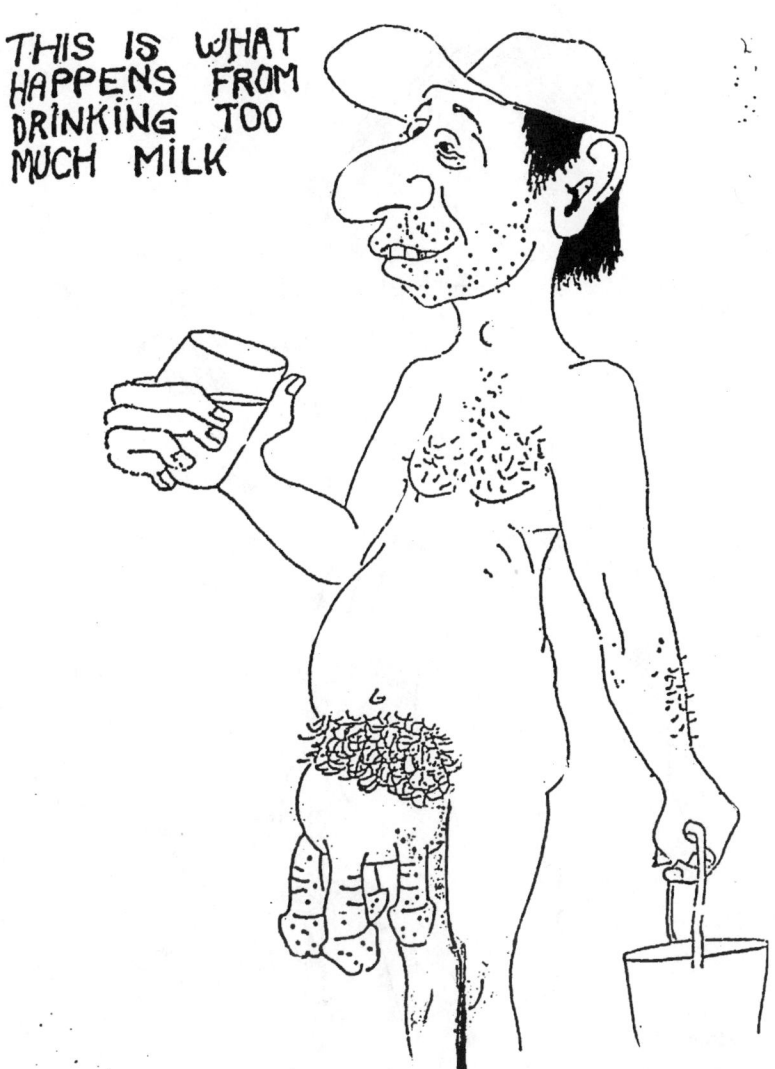

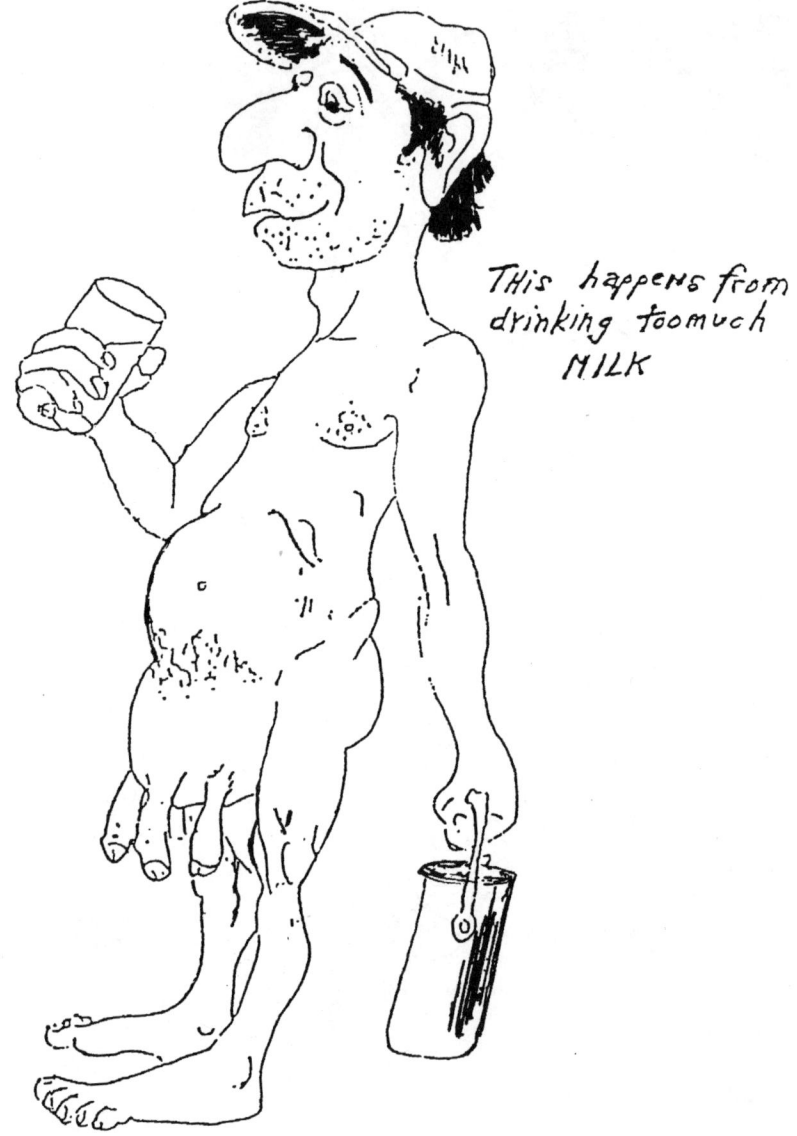

128. A "Cow" Boy

One additional item again confirms the phallic-udder tradition. A literalization of the term "cowboy" transforms a male into a bovine troubadour. The first version was collected in Seattle in 1981, the second from Virginia in 1990. The variations include the feather in the hat, the straw or cigarette in the mouth, the presence of a bottle, and the movement of the guitar, among other details. A version, reported in Sweden, is titled "Milk drinkers are better lovers" (MF, 101, #81).

A "Cow" boy.

129. Stuffing the Turkey

In the folklore of animals, there is some consideration of the taboo subject of bestiality. It may be difficult for some readers to accept the notion that some individuals, male and female, engage in sexual acts with various animals. For considerations of this topic, see G. Dubois-Desaulle, *Étude sur la Bestialité au point de vue Historique, Médical et Juridique* (Paris: Charles Carrington, 1905) and RDJ, 206–16.

The following cartoon was collected in north-central Pennsylvania in 1990. The caption refers, ostensibly, to a grandfather of a family helping to prepare the traditional Thanksgiving turkey. However, the verb "to stuff," as in "get stuffed," means to get screwed, and "bird" can be a slang term for a young woman. A turkey is, of course, a type of bird, and the allusion to a turkey as a bird is confirmed by a Thanksgiving parody sung to the tune of "Frere Jacques":

>Next Thanksgiving, Next Thanksgiving
>
>Save Your Bread, Save Your Bread
>
>Stuff it up a turkey, Stuff it up a turkey
>
>Eat the bird, Eat the bird.

Offbeat Beasthood 243

130. The Italian Lover

Bestiality occurs much more often with animals such as cows, horses, and sheep rather than turkeys. In theory, a male having intercourse with an animals is using that animal as a substitute for a woman. Presumably, a male would prefer a human female to a domestic animal. In the following traditional cartoon, a misguided male has relations with a donkey instead of with the woman supine on the back of the animal. The first version, from Montgomery, Alabama, in 1991, shows an Italian protagonist—Italians are stereotypically regarded as great lovers, part of the Latin Lover image—singing the classic aria "O Sole Mio," but the misspelling of "Sole" as "Solo" underscores the fact that he is operating "solo," that is, without a human female partner. The second version was collected in Hayward, California in 1987; the third from San Francisco in 1976; the fourth from New Zealand in 1991; while the last version appears to be an updating of the image, insofar as a motorcycle has replaced the donkey. It was collected in Berkeley in 1981. The variation is quite extraordinary as one can easily observe by comparing the carriages, the expressions on the donkeys' faces, and the captions, among other facets of the drawings.

There are oral jokes involving the placement of the male organ in the "wrong hole." For a text in which a western cowboy beds a female Indian who shouts "Wahoo" during the act, see NLM, 165. In the denouement, she reveals to him that "Wahoo" means "wrong hole."

Offbeat Beasthood 245

131. Stop Crying Mary

In jokes, the favorite animal for bestial acts is clearly the sheep. (For typical texts, see RDJ, 209–10). Virgin wool, for example, is defined as wool from a sheep that can run faster than the shepherd. Perhaps the most famous nursery rhyme in the English language is "Mary had a little lamb" (see Iona and Peter Opie, *The Oxford Dictionary of Nursery Rhymes* (Oxford: Univ. Press, 1951), 299–300. The following item was collected in Savage, Minnesota, in August 1994, and it assumes the reader's familiarity with the poetic staple that has inspired a massive number of parodies over the years, e.g., Mary had a little lamb—the doctor fainted. See also C. Grant Loomis, "Mary Had A Parody: A Rhyme of Childhood in Folk Tradition," *Western Folklore*, 17 (1958), 45–51.

"Stop crying Mary, you're next."

132. The Line-Up

In criminal cases of rape and other felonies, the victim is often asked to identify her assailant from a group of individuals assembled in a specially designed room that permits her to view them through a one-way glass window. The assemblage is commonly termed a "line-up." In the following item from Savage, Minnesota, in 1994, the victimized sheep is sitting on a bench about to pick out the farmer who violated her.

133. The Shepherd

Even though humans cannot produce offspring through bestial acts, the folk imagination has no such impediment. The following item, which was part of a large collection of photocopier folklore from Lancashire, England, in 1978, portrays the possible results of a shepherd's activity with his flock. This item is somewhat unusual insofar as it bears an attribution, namely, to Michael Jupp.

The shepherd's alleged proclivity to do more than vocalize "I love ewe," is also demonstrated in a traditional folk poem titled, "The Shepherd's Serenade." The following version was collected in Washington, D.C. in April 1976.

>Here's to the sheepherder who sleeps in the grass
>With his well trained dog curled up at his ass.
>An old ewe stands licking his balls
>That hang thru a rip in his overalls.
>The magpie sits in a tree nearby
>Scanning the scene with a watchful eye.
>The sheepherder awoke from his blissful sleep.
>And immediately began to screw the sheep.
>The dog barked and the sheepherder quit,
>The sheep bleated and the magpie shit.

250 *Why Don't Sheep Shrink When It Rains?*

134. Italian Duck Call

Man's relationship to animals includes both domestic and wild varieties. Contact with the latter typically involves hunting, a pastime that has produced a wealth of folklore ranging from superstititions to tall tales. (See, for example, the section of "Hunting Tales" in the Aarne-Thompson tale type index, AT 1890–1909.)

Two of the most common quarries are ducks and deer. In duck hunting, the hunters normally hide in what is termed a "blind." This conceals the hunters from the ducks' view. In order to attract the fowl, hunters may resort to using one of several artifices. Examples of such aids are wooden replicas of floating ducks, that is, "decoys," and devices engineered to imitate the sounds made by ducks. These "duck calls" are a type of whistle that is blown into by the hunters to produce what is supposed to imitate a duck's squawk or quack.

The following cartoon makes fun of this practice by portraying a hunter encouraging a live duck, in an imaginative way, to produce the desired call. To the extent that the cartoon attributes dumbness to the hunter, it provides an opportunity for an ethnic joke. The most common title of this cartoon is "Italian Duck Call," but in some versions it is a Polish duck call. The first version was collected in Winnipeg in 1980; the second in Lafayette, California in 1999. The third and fourth versions show that the slur can be applied equally to rival colleges and universities. The third version, collected in San Antonio, Texas, in 1983, is part of the larger Texas Aggie joke cycle, which has as its perennial victims students and graduates of Agricultural and Mechanical University. (For other Aggie folklore, see SD, 87–88). The fourth version, collected in Montgomery, Alabama, in 1991, substitutes Auburn as the college target, presumably from the perspective of arch-rival University of Alabama.

The variation exhibited in these three versions is considerable. One need only consider the poses and faces of the dogs, the angle of the guns, the wings and heads of the duck, the foliage, etc. On the other hand, there are enough details in common, e.g., the beanie with the propeller and the general configuration of the dog, duck, and hunter, to clearly point to cognation. For another version, titled "Polish Duck Call," see UFFC-PC, 30.

Offbeat Beasthood 253

AGGIE DUCK CALL

135. Miss America Duck Call

Duck hunting is normally regarded as an all-male activity. Women's presence on hunting expeditions is rare to say the least. However, the following cartoon has transformed the duck call image into a parody of an all-female event. The annual Miss America pageant, the finals of which are televised nationwide and beyond, pits representatives from states and territories in a somewhat grueling competition involving beauty, talent, and poise. To the extent that there may be an unconscious, underlying homoerotic aspect to all-male hunting groups, this theme has been projected onto an all-female group.

The cartoon, collected in Savage, Minnesota, in 1994, implies a Lesbian element exists in the Miss America festival. The pseudo-address contains a number of obscene puns referring to analinctus. According to a brief note accompanying a version of this cartoon appearing in *Maledicta* 8 (1984–85), 224, the cartoon was inspired by events involving Vanessa Williams, the first African American women to be crowned Miss America. This occurred in 1984.

Two months before the end of her one-year reign as Miss America, Vanessa Williams was forced to resign because nude pictures of her were published in *Penthouse* magazine. Apparently at the tender age of 19, she had taken a summer job in a local photography studio in her hometown of Millwood, New York. There she was persuaded to allow a photographer to take pictures of her nude. In one session, she was photographed with a white woman. Although she had been assured that the pictures would never be released, they were and the resultant scandal cost her the Miss America crown. Happily, Williams has been able to overcome this unfortunate episode to enjoy a career as a successful actress and singer.

ORDER YOURS TODAY!!
Miss America Duck Call

BACKDOOR ENTERPRISES
Box #2
Brownhole, Miss.

136. Fetch the Duck

In duck hunting, the hunter often sends his faithful dog to retrieve the fallen bird. In the following cartoon, collected on the ship Glomar Challenger, in 1971, the dog is depicted as having misunderstood the hunter's command. The mistake may allude to a common rhyming expression, "Fuck-a-Duck." For a discussion of this phrase, see Jesse Sheidlower, *The F Word* (New York: Random House, 1995), 55, 115–16. See also RDJ, 178.

137. Dear Diary

Part of the pleasure in hunting duck or deer is getting away from the urban scene to enjoy the beauties of nature. The same motivation may lead individuals to move to a different part of the country in search of a pastoral paradise. However, sometimes reality intrudes, and Eden turns out to be flawed.

The following traditional item, known from coast to coast, makes passing reference to deer in the most common version. The first text, collected in Berkeley, California, in July 1996, is set in Pennsylvania, but other versions (not presented here) are placed in Connecticut, New Jersey, New York, Vermont, and Virginia. A second version, collected in Santa Ana, California, in January 1997, does not refer to a specific locale. It is titled "A Westerner Moves East" (and an alternative title is "A Southerner Moves Up North"). A third version, "Snow," was collected in Downsville, New York in July 1996. Despite considerable variation in these three versions, there are some striking commonalities, e.g., the gradual progression from idyllic contentment to nightmarish exasperation, and the increasing vilification of the snowplow driver. For a version titled "Winter Wonderland," see FOJ2, 492.

DEAR DIARY

August 12: Moved to our new home in Pennsylvania. It is so beautiful here. The mountains are so majestic. Can hardly wait to see them covered with snow. I love it here.

October 14: Pennsylvania is the most beautiful place on earth. The leaves are turned all the colors and shades of orange and red. Went for a ride through the beautiful mountains and saw some deer. They are so graceful, certainly the most wonderful animals on earth. This must be paradise. I love it here.

November 11: Deer season will start soon. I cannot imagine anyone wanting to kill such a gorgeous creature. I hope it will snow soon. I love it here.

December 2: It snowed all night. Woke up to find everything blanketed with white. It looks like a postcard. We went outside and cleaned the snow off the steps and shoveled the driveway. We had a snowball fight (I won) and when the snowplow came by, we had to shovel the driveway again. What a beautiful place, I love Pennsylvania.

December 10: More snow last night. Could not get out of the driveway to get to work. I am exhausted from shoveling. Fucking snow plow.

December 22: More of that white shit fell last night. I have got blisters on my hands from shoveling. I think the snow plow hides around the corner and waits until I am done shoveling the driveway. Asshole.

December 25: Merry Fucking Christmas! More friggin' snow. If I ever get my hands on that son-of-a-bitch who drives the snow plow, I swear I will kill the bastard. Do not know why they do not use more salt on the roads to melt the fucking ice.

December 27: More white shit last night. Been inside for 3 days except for shoveling out the driveway after the snow plow goes through every time. Cannot go anywhere. Car is stuck in a mountain of white shit. The weatherman says to expect another 10 inches of the shit again tonight. Do you know how many shovel's-full of snow 10 inches is?

December 28: The fucking weatherman was wrong. We got 34 inches of that white shit this time. At this rate, it will not melt before next summer. The snow plow got stuck up the road and that bastard came to my door and asked to borrow my shovel. I told him that I had broken six shovels already shoveling all the shit he pushed into my driveway. I broke the last one over his fucking head.

January 4: Finally got out of the house today. Went to the store to get some food and on the way back a damned deer ran in front of the car and I hit it. Did about $3,000 damage to the car. Those fucking beasts should be killed. Wish the hunters had killed them all last summer.

May 3: Took the car to the garage in town. Would you believe the thing is rusted out from all the fucking salt they put all over the road?

May 10: Moved to Florida. I cannot imagine why anyone in their right mind would ever live in that God-forsaken state of Pennsylvania.

A WESTERNER MOVES EAST

JAN 10, 5:00 pm—It's starting to snow. The first of the season and the first one we've seen in years. The wife and I took our hot buttered rums and sat by the picture windows, watching the soft flakes drift down, clinging to the trees and covering the ground. It was beautiful.

JAN 11 We awoke to a lovely blanket of crystal white snow covering the landscape. What a fantastic sight. Every tree and shrub covered with a beautiful white mantle. I shoveled snow for the first time in years and loved it. I did both our driveway and our sidewalk. Later the city snowplow came and accidentally covered up our driveway with compacted snow from the street. The driver smiled and waved. I waved back and shoveled it again.

JAN 12 It snowed an additional 5 inches last night and the temperature has dropped to about 12 degrees. Several limbs on the trees and shrubs snapped due to the weight of the snow. I shoveled our driveway again. Shortly afterwards the snowplow came by and did his trick again. Much of the snow is now brownish and gray.

JAN 13 Warmed up enough during the day to create some slush which soon became ice when the temperature dropped again. Bought snow tires for both cars. Fell on my ass in the driveway. $145 to a chiropractor, but nothing was broken. More snow and ice expected.

JAN 14 Still cold. Sold the wife's car and bought a 4 x 4 in order to get to work. Slid into guard-rail anyway and did a considerable amount of damage to the right quarter panel. Had another 8 inches of white shit last night. Both vehicles covered in salt and crud. More shoveling in store for me today. That goddam snowplow came by twice today.

JAN 15 2 degrees outside. More fuckin' snow. Not a tree or shrub on our property that hasn't been damaged. Power was off most of the night. Tried to keep from freezing to death with candles and a kerosene heater, which tipped over and nearly burned the house down. I managed to put the flames out but suffered 2nd degree burns on my hands and lost all my eye lashes and eyebrows. Car slid on the ice on the way to the emergency room and was totaled.

JAN 16 Goddam mother fuckin' white shit keeps coming down. Have put all the clothes on we own just to get to the fuckin' mailbox. If I ever catch that son-of-a-bitch that drives the snowplow I'll chew open his chest and rip out his heart. I think he hides around the corner and waits to plow shut our driveway again!

JAN 17 Six goddam more fuckin' inches of fuckin' snow and fuckin' sleet and fuckin' ice and god knows what other kind of white fuckin' shit fell last night. I wounded the fuckin' snowplow asshole with an ice ax, but he got away. Wife left me. Car won't start. I think I'm snowblind. I can't move my toes. Haven't seen the sun in weeks. More snow predicted. Windchill—12 fuckin' degrees below zero. I'm moving back to California.

SNOW

Dec 8 — 6:00 pm. It's started to snow. The first of the season and the wife and I took our cocktails, and sat by the window watching the soft flakes drift down all over the area. It was BEAUTIFUL!

Dec 9 — We awoke to a big beautiful blanket of crystal white snow covering the landscape. What a fantastic sight. Every tree and shrub covered with a beautiful white mantle. I shoveled snow for the first time in years and loved it. I did both our driveway and our sidewalk. Later the snowplow came along and covered up our sidewalk with compacted snow from the street, so I shoveled it again.

Dec 12 — The sun has melted all our lovely snow. Oh, well, I'm sure we will get some more before this lovely winter is through.

Dec 14 — It snowed 8 inches last night and the temperature dropped to 20 degrees below zero. Shoveled the driveway and sidewalk again and the snowplow came by and did its trick again.

Dec. 15 — Sold my van and bought a 4 X 4 Jeep so I can drive through the snow. Bought snow tires for my wife's car. Had to get deicer for door locks and gas cap locks before we could use our keys.

Dec 16 — Fell on my ass on the ice in the driveway. All that was hurt was my feelings.

Dec 17 — It's the wife's birthday today and the icy roads make for very tough driving. I walked to the corner gas station and got her a set of tire chains and an ice scraper. Wrapped them in Christmas paper, but she was happy.

Dec 20 — Still cold (below zero in AM). Had another 14 inches of the white shit last night. More shoveling in store for me today. That damn snowplow came by twice.

Dec 22 — We are assured of a white Christmas because 13 more inches of the white shit fell today, and with the freezing weather, it won't melt until August. Got all dressed up to go out and shovel (boots, jumpsuit, heavy jacket, scarf, earmuffs, gloves, etc.) and then I got the urgent need to pee!

Dec 23   I was going to go ice fishing today but my worms were outside and I didn't want the fish to break their teeth on my bait.

Dec 24   If I ever catch the son-of-a-bitch that drives that snowplow, I'll drag him through the snow by his balls. I think he hides around the corner and waits for me to finish shoveling and then he comes down the street at 100 miles an hour and throws snow all over what used to be my lawn.

Dec 25   Merry Christmas! They predict 28 more inches of the fucking white stuff tonight. Do they know how many shovels-full 28 inches is? To Hell with Santa. He doesn't have to shovel that shit. The snowplow driver came by asking for a donation. I grabbed my snow shovel, but he ran before I could hit him with it.

Dec 26   We got 28 inches and then some. I must be going snow-blind or have a severe case of cabin fever because the wife is beginning to look good to me.

Dec 27   The toilet froze. If you go outside, don't eat any colored snow.

Dec 28   I set fire to the house. At least that white shit won't cling to the roof anymore!

138. The Deer Hunt

Deerhunting proper may also involve a clear distinction between fantasy or the ideal on the one hand, and the more mundane frustrations of reality on the other. The following item, collected in Foster City, California, in 1986, uses the device of progression to underscore that distinction. In this instance, the day starts badly and get steadily worse. For another version, see FOJ, 211.

THE DEER HUNT

Saturday
1:00 A.M.	Alarm clock rings
2:00	Hunting partner arrives, drags you out of bed
2:30	Throw everything except the kitchen sink in truck
3:00	Leave for deep woods
3:15	Drive back home and pick up gun
3:30	Drive like hell to get to woods before daylight
4:00	Set up camp; forgot damn tent
4:30	Head into the woods
6:05	See 8 deer
6:06	Take aim and squeeze trigger
6:07	"CLICK"
6:08	Load gun while watching 8 deer go over hill
8:00	Head back to camp
9:00	Still looking for camp
10:00	Realize you don't know where camp is
Noon	Fire gun for help—eat wild berries
12:15 P.M.	Ran out of bullets—8 deer came back
12:20	Strange feeling in stomach
12:30	Realize you ate poison berries
12:45	Rescued!!
12:55	Rushed to hospital to have stomach pumped
3:00	Arrive back at camp
3:30	Leave camp to kill deer
4:00	Return to camp for bullets
4:01	Load gun—leave camp again
5:00	Empty gun on squirrel that's bugging you
6:00	Arrive at camp, see deer grazing in camp
6:01	Load gun
6:02	Fire gun
6:03	One dead truck

6:05	Hunting partner returns to camp dragging deer
6:06	Repress strong desire to shoot partner
6:07	Fell in fire
6:10	Change clothes throw burned ones into fire
6:15	Take truck, leave partner and his deer in woods
6:25	Truck boils over—hole shot in block
6:26	Start walking
6:30	Stumble and fall, drop gun in mud
6:35	Meet bear
6:36	Take aim
6:37	Fire gun—blow up barrel plugged with mud
6:38	Shit pants
6:39	Climb tree
9:00	Bear departs—wrap gun around tree
Midnight	Home at last
Sunday	Watch football game on TV, slowly tearing license into little pieces. Place in envelope and mail to Game Warden with clear instructions on where to place it............

139. Basic Rules for Deer Hunting

The previous litany of things that can go wrong in a deer hunting expedition are more succinctly articulated in the following item, collected in Castro Valley, California in August 1973. The ever-present danger of shooting something other than a deer—including other hunters—is greatly magnified by the excessive consumption of alcohol by members of the hunting party. The particulars of the list of provisions, plus the allusion to "pink elephants," emphasize the potentially lethal combination of guns and alcohol.

BASIC RULES FOR DEER HUNTING

7-day provisions:

Standard per person: 7 bottles of whisky, 3 six-packs of beer and a bottle of aspirin. Emergency provision per person: 2 six-packs of beer (or a bottle of whisky), 1 loaf of bread, 3-4 bullets.

1. Always bring a rifle.
2. Shoot any moving object. It could be a Deer.
3. Never use a red hat or clothes with strong colors. It upsets mother nature.
4. Never bring a dog. It could get shot. Leave the hunting to one of your buddies.
5. If you forget your rifle and meet a Deer, hide in the bushes.
6. If you see pink elephants, don't bother. Pink elephants don't exist. Shoot anyway.
7. Always bring a photo or a drawing of a Deer. Cows and horses are rapidly diminishing in our country.
8. Have a daily count of your buddies to see how many are left.

HAPPY HUNTING!

140. I think I Just Heard a Buck Snort!

Another downside aspect of roughing it in the woods is answering the call of nature. Far away from modern plumbing and the comforts of toilet tissue, one must make do as best one can. With trigger-happy hunting companions, one takes a risk in going off by oneself for whatever reason. The following cartoon was collected in north-central Pennsylvania, in 1990, from a female secretary.

"Quiet—I think I just heard a buck snort!"

141. Here's Your Deer Meat

Folklore fantasy often indulges in reversals of reality. Instead of men attacking deer, deer may attack men. The following cartoons purport to present hunting from a deer's perspective. The play on such words as "meat" and "sausage" provides an angry deer an opportunity to sodomize his hunter antagonist. The first version was collected in Downsville, New York in July 1996; the second was collected from a member of a duck club in the Sacramento-San Joaquin rivers' delta in February 1992; the third was collected in Clairton, Pennsylvania in January 1976. In the third version, the macho deer takes revenge for the hunter's indiscriminate killing of does, that is, his females. Presumably, since there is a hunter-caused shortage of female deer companions, the male deer has no other outlet for his sexual drives than the hunter. The cartoon affords a rare chance for bestiality in reverse.

142. This One's Barely Legal!!

In hunting and fishing regulations, which vary from state to state, there are, inevitably, restrictions with respect to size and gender. Fish under the size limit are supposed to be released; in some states, it is forbidden to shoot does out of season, or, in some cases, to shoot them at all.

The following folk cartoon again demonstrates a striking role reversal, with the deer taking on the role of hunter and men serving as the hunted. The allusion to size is explicitly phallic, which strongly suggests that hunters and fishermen who brag about the size of their catch may have similar underpinnings.

The first version was collected in 1990 from a store clerk in north-central Pennsylvania. The second version was collected in Savage, Minnesota, in August 1994, and it is of particular interest because it includes a female human with a "doe permit" attached to her toe (just as identifying labels are attached to corpses in morgues!). The third version, which is more graphic, was collected in Downsville, New York, in July 1996. It is distinctive in having three deer and what appears to be a vulture perched on a tree limb awaiting a feast. Those not familiar with deer hunting may not realize that deer, once killed, are normally hung from a tree limb to drain them of blood and to facilitate gutting them.

143. Fisherman's Prayer

Fishing is just as popular as hunting, if not more so. The issue of size, with respect to whether or not a particular fish is a "keeper," becomes transformed into a quasi-religious sentiment in the following text collected from Savage, Minnesota in August 1994. In this case, it is not a fish that causes a role reversal, but rather a human who intentionally perceives himself as a fish hoping to be considered worthy of entering heaven. The metaphor is an old one. In Matthew 4:19, Jesus tells Simon-called-Peter and Andrew, his brother, both of whom were fisherman, to follow him, and he would make them "fishers of men." For other photocopier texts involving fishing, see NT, 59–60, and SD, 188–93.

FISHERMAN'S PRAYER

I pray that I may
live to fish until my
dying day.

And when it comes to
my last cast, I then
most humbly pray;

When in the Lord's
great landing net
and peacefully asleep

That in His mercy
I be judged - - - - - - -

BIG ENOUGH TO KEEP.

Pictorial Picks

Folk cartoons continue to be one of the most prominent and imaginative forms of photocopier folklore. Cartoons more effectively encapsulate ideas and more forcefully articulate them than mere texts alone possibly can. Many are accompanied by captions, but in the end, it is the drawings that are most telling. In a few cases, we have included items that are not cartoons, but which are thematically related to cartoons. We feel that it is fitting to conclude this volume with some of the very best examples of the folk cartoon genre.

144. There Must Be More to Life

It is mistakenly believed that technology kills folklore, but the truth is that technology has itself spawned its own folklore. The very agent of photocopier transmission, that is, the photocopier, has become a character in modern folklore. In the following folk cartoon, collected in Morgantown, West Virginia, in November 1996, a copy machine is musing about the nature of life. The name-plate of the machine contains the phrase "Copies R Us," a parody of the Toys-R-Us retail chain. The question asked is actually a very profound human one. Is there more to life than breeding and dying? A goodly portion of the discipline of philosophy is devoted to the consideration of this basic question. For another photocopier treatment of xerographic reproduction, see NT, 339–41.

145. Jammed Again

In theory, technology is designed to facilitate human activities, to make life easier and simpler. In fact, technology can frustrate the best of human efforts. By becoming more and more dependent upon technology, humans run the risk of losing individual skills and self-reliance. In the following folk cartoon, collected in North Haven, Connecticut, in July 1996, a would-be user of the copy machine has been totally ingested by it. His hands are shown emerging, still clutching the sheet of paper he had hoped to copy. For other examples of technological breakdown, see SD, 2–4, 6–7.

"This crazy thing is jammed again."

146. The Computer Broke Down

When technology fails, humans are forced to rely on their own resources. In some instances, it has been so long since certain human skills were actually put to use that the humans in question are no longer able to carry out even the simplest tasks. The dangers of becoming overly dependent upon computers and their technological brethren is the subject of the following folk cartoon collected in Savage, Minnesota in August 1994. The depiction of the group in the room behind a door marked "Control" is a telling one. They share a single desk, a desk that is virtually bare. Their body postures suggest they are not doing anything and that they probably haven't done anything for some time. The picture on the wall of the founder seems to match the image of the man on the far left. If this is so, even the founder is shown to have little or nothing further to contribute to his company.

The computer broke down. Anyone here have experience in thinking?

147. Who's Got the Brain Today?

In an era when individuals are not encouraged to think, thinking may become burdensome. It is easier to appoint someone to do the thinking required, similar to selecting a "designated driver" to stay sober in order to drive a group home safely. So the question of the day in an office might well be, "Who's going to do the thinking for us today?" The following item was collected in Iselin, New Jersey in April 1997.

148. Burned Out

Some jobs require such dedication, energy, and intense effort that it becomes difficult to sustain enthusiasm over an extended period of time. Very high stress occupations, often involving life and death situations, may take their toll on the individuals engaged in them. The state of being utterly exhausted, drained, and no longer interested in one's life work is termed "burn out." The following folk cartoon, collected in Logan, Utah, in April 1992, provides a dramatic literalization of that popular metaphor.

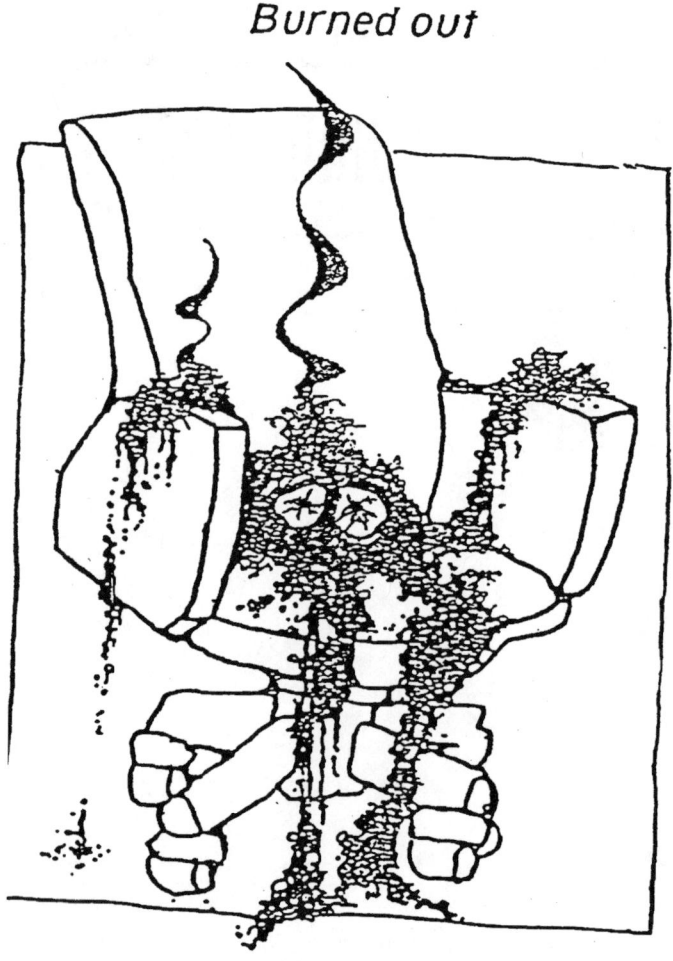

149. Tired of Your Job???

One of the causes of "burn out" is a growing disenchantment with one's job or profession. If the job is no longer challenging and has become a mind-dulling daily routine, one may be tempted to make a career change or to move to another location. The following item is a parody of the desire to change jobs, poking fun at what is perceived to be runaway welfare benefits available in certain states, e.g., California (and in some versions New York). The first version was collected in Walnut Creek, California in 1994; the second is from Berkeley, also in 1994. These two versions have similar content, but quite different formats. The third item was collected in Albany, California in November 1977. It is thematically related to the first two texts. For another traditional commentary on the welfare state, see WH, 171–73.

TIRED OF YOUR JOB ??

Sick of Working 40 hours or more each week just to feed your family

Would you like to relax all day and still have all the benefits of a full-time job ?

If you answered yes to any of these questions You should consider moving to:

CALIFORNIA
"THE WELFARE STATE"

If you qualify(and only working people don't), you can receive the following:

FREE HOUSING
FREE UTILITIES
FREE FOOD
FREE MEDICAL INSURANCE(No Limits)
FREE CASH (For cigarettes, Beer, Dope, etc.)
FREE TRANSPORTATION
FREE LEGAL SERVICES

This program is not limited to 3 to 6 months like other states. In California you can collect for life. Some of our families have received benefits for two or three generations !

So, if you would like to receive all of this without working for a living, just call The California Department of Social Services at: 1-800-FREELOAD (Even the Call is Free !!)

TIRED OF YOUR JOB???

SICK OF WORKING 40 HRS OR MORE EACH WEEK JUST TO FEED YOUR FAMILY? WOULD YOU LIKE TO RELAX ALL DAY AND STILL HAVE ALL THE BENEFITS OF A FULL TIME JOB? IF YOU HAVE ANSWERED YES TO ANY OF THESE QUESTIONS, YOU SHOULD CONSIDER MOVING TO...

CALIFORNIA!

"THE WELFARE STATE!"

IF YOU QUALIFY, (AND ONLY WORKING PEOPLE DON'T), YOU COULD RECEIVE THE FOLLOWING:

FREE HOUSING - FREE UTILITIES
FREE FOOD - FREE TELEVISION
FREE MEDICAL INSURANCE & HOSPITAL
FREE TRANSPORTATION AND
LEGAL SERVICES - FREE METHADONE
AND FREE CASH FOR CIGARETTES,
BEER, DRUGS, LOTTERY, ETC.

THIS PROGRAM IS NOT LIMITED TO 3 OR 6 MONTHS LIKE OTHER STATES. IN CALIFORNIA, YOU CAN COLLECT FOR LIFE! SOME OF OUR FAMILIES HAVE RECEIVED BENEFITS FOR TWO, AND THREE GENERATIONS, AND THEY ARE STILL RECEIVING.

SO, IF YOU WOULD LIKE TO RECEIVE ALL OF THIS WITHOUT WORKING FOR A LIVING, JUST CALL THE CALIFORNIA DEPARTMENT OF SOCIAL SERVICES... THEY CAN HELP.

THE NUMBER IS
1-800-FREELOAD
(SEE, EVEN THE CALL IS FREE)

150. Greetings from California

California may have the image of the ideal welfare state, but it also has some drawbacks. Perhaps the principal negative feature of life in California is the constant threat of a severe earthquake. Californians themselves have learned for the most part to take earthquakes in stride. Hence, the following folk cartoon shows a parody of a greeting card in which either native Californians or visiting tourists are making light of a quake in progress. It was collected in Baltimore, Maryland in 1994.

151. Please, Do Go on with Your Story

Hard luck stories are often told to gain sympathy from listeners. However, some audiences soon tire of hearing such stories. A common gesture, functioning as a proverb indicating that one is not impressed with the sad story being told, consists of a violin-bowing movement, sometimes accompanied by singing the initial portion of a melody titled "Hearts and Flowers," or a similar overly saccharine, sentimental song. The following folk cartoon alludes to this gesture and musical tradition. The first version was collected in Fort Worth, Texas, in 1965, while the second was collected in Las Vegas, Nevada in 1994.

Please, do go on with your story. . .

152. Let Go Me Ankles, Murphy

A group that is often the subject of ethnic slurs in England and the United States is the Irish. (For a useful consideration of ethnic slurs, see Christie Davies, *Ethnic Humor Around the World: A Comparative Analysis* (Bloomington: Indiana Univ. Press, 1990.) The following folk cartoon was collected in Oakland, California, in 1974, at a business establishment whose name included "Murphy." A second version (not presented here), collected in 1981 from a man named Murphy, bears a caption: "Communicate & Cooperate, Boys—Or Else Both Fall!"

153. Thermometers in the Refrigerator

Jokes about stupidity are not confined to ethnic groups. There is the subject of occupational stupidity as well. In the following folk cartoon, collected in Wilmington, Delaware, in December 1990, a patient is in some distress that could easily have been avoided. There is a doctor-nurse dialogue in which an aloof doctor offers an obvious piece of advice to an apparently surprised nurse. The cartoon provides a commentary on the perceived ineptitude of some hospital personnel.

"That wouldn't happen if you'd stop storing those thermometers in the refrigerator."

154. In Order to Speed Your Recovery

There are modern means of taking a patient's temperature, e.g., with a thimble-like device placed over a patient's finger. However, in times past, temperatures were taken either by mouth or rectally. The following greeting card parody uses a phallic instrument for the alleged measurement of body temperature. The normal temperature of 98.6 requires near full insertion. This text was collected at Sacramento State University in 1979.

155. Your Bedpan, Sir!!

Temperature-taking may be a mildly annoying necessity in a hospital, but it pales when compared to carrying out procedures for the elimination of body wastes. Nonambulatory patients, confined to bed, are obliged to utilize bedpans in order to defecate. The following traditional folk cartoon, which spans at least fifty years, portrays an aggressively unsympathetic nurse manhandling a supine patient. The first two versions are from ISR and dated 1947. The third version was collected from a Howard County courthouse maintenance man in Kokomo, Indiana in October 1976. The fourth version was collected in New Zealand in April 1994. The fifth version is from Kokomo, Indiana, in August 1976, while the sixth and final version was collected in Downsville, New York in July 1996.

Our aim in presenting a half-dozen versions of this item is to demonstrate its remarkable combination of stability and variation through time. While the basic image is stable, the captions, utterances of the distraught patient, and body postures reflect considerable variation. For an account of a version dating from 1952, see NLM, 462–63.

Why Don't Sheep Shrink When It Rains?

Pictorial Picks   291

"I'M So NERVOUS, THIS IS MY FIRST DAY ON THE WARDS!"

156. Hillary Clinton Health Care Reform

Early in President Bill Clinton's first term, shortly after his inauguration in January 1993, he appointed his wife Hillary to head a task force charged with reforming the nation's troubled health care system. It was a laudable goal, but Mrs. Clinton was not an elected official, and she had no particular expertise in health care. The proposal, which ultimately failed to gain congressional support, was widely criticized, in part because of the public's perception that medical care was going to be greatly curtailed. This perception is clearly reflected in the following popular folk cartoon. The first version was collected at Meris Labs, a medical testing facility in Berkeley on Christmas Day, 1993; the second was collected at Kaiser Vallejo (California) Hospital in the spring of 1993. Our earliest version (not presented here) was collected in Virginia, in March 1993, not long after the task force was created.

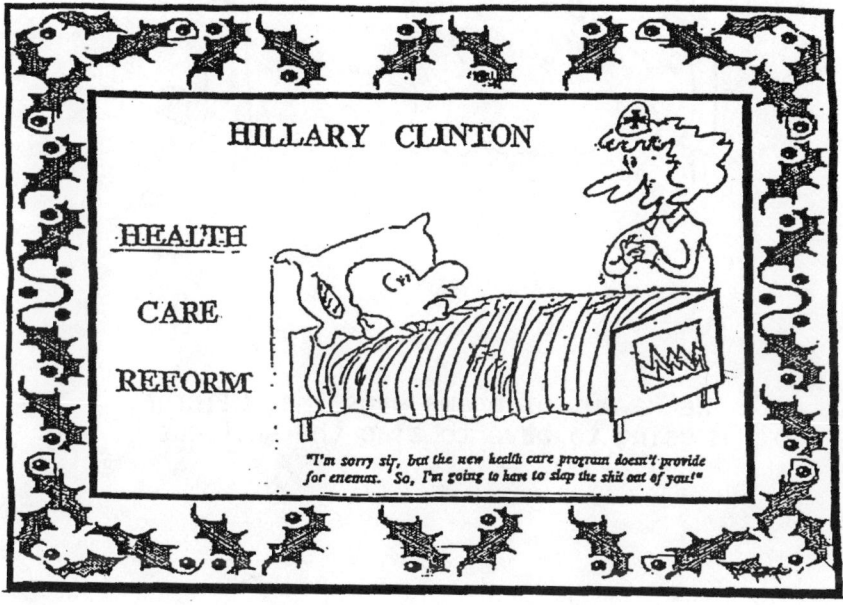

AFTER
Hillary's Health Care Reform

We're out of enema bags, Mr. Clinton.
So I'm going to have to slap the shit out of you.

157. Mothers!!

The phrase "beating the shit out of someone" is a metaphor for imposing severe physical punishment upon an individual. It is not normally understood literally as a medical procedure. The following card from ISR plays upon the contrast between literal and metaphorical feces, as did the previous item.

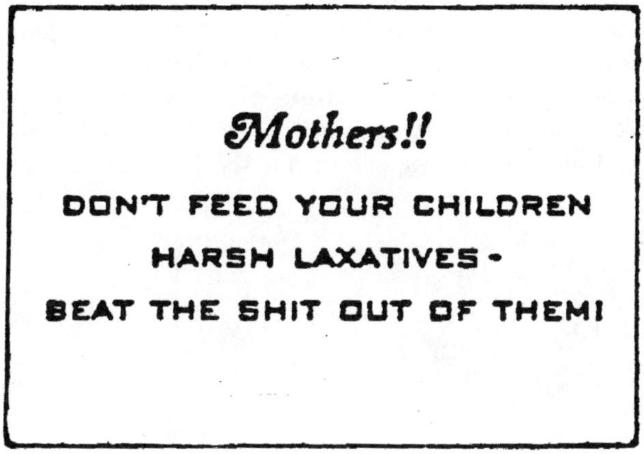

Mothers!!
DON'T FEED YOUR CHILDREN
HARSH LAXATIVES -
BEAT THE SHIT OUT OF THEM!

158. The Birth of a Salesman

Salesmen unfortunately enjoy a poor reputation as being unpleasant, pushy, and downright dishonest, willing to do almost anything to sell their product. The following folk cartoon, from Fairfield, California, in April 1995, reveals the public's negative attitude toward salesmen. A "horse's ass" is a standard idiom for someone pompous and full of himself. "Horseshit" is a common synonym for something useless or valueless (cf. "Bullshit"). In this cartoon, salesmen are shown emerging as fully-formed turds born with cigars in their mouths and ready to glad-hand anyone they meet. They are also depicted as being all alike. There may or may not be an allusion (in the item's title) to Arthur Miller's 1949 Pulitzer prize-winning play *Death of a Salesman*. For other photocopier folklore treating salesmen, see NT, 228–29, 243, 278–79.

159. No! I Can't Be Bothered

In fairness to salesmen, sometimes they actually have a "better mousetrap" that the consumer ignores at his peril. An *a priori* refusal to hear out a salesman's pitch may prove to be a fatal mistake. The following folk cartoon makes this point in dramatic fashion. Its subtext might also hint at the dependence upon arms sales for economic prosperity.

The first version was collected in Pleasant Hill, California, in 1980, while the second and third versions were collected in Chicago in March 1994. The diversity of images in these three versions is a testament to the creativity of the folk. The text, in contrast, exhibits much less variation.

"NO!- I CAN'T BE BOTHERED TO SEE ANY CRAZY SALESMEN- WE'VE GOT A BATTLE TO FIGHT!"

160. Air Bag

One of the new gadgets sold to American automobile owners is the air bag, an inflatable sack that explosively fills with air if and when a vehicle experiences a sudden impact. Air bags emerge from the steering wheel on the driver's side or the dashboard near the glove compartment on the front-seat passenger's side. The following folk cartoon shows a man caught in a compromising position using the pretense of being hit in the face with an air bag as an excuse to an investigating police officer. The first version was collected in Walnut Creek, California, in March 1995, the second in San Francisco in January 1996.

161. Are You Sure That's a Breathalizer?

The police are not always portrayed as guardians of moral virtue. In the following folk cartoon, it is a policeman who seeks to initiate a sexual encounter. The cartoon refers to another modern invention, this one being a scientific means of gauging a driver's blood alcohol content by testing his breath expelled into a balloon. This gadget, commonly termed a "breathalizer," is administered by an officer suspicious of an erratic driver. (In California, a motorist is given a choice of options: urine test, blood test, or breathalizer.)

The first version was collected in Wilmington, Delaware in December 1990; the second from Iselin, New Jersey in July 1995; the third from Chicago, in March 1994; and the fourth from Savage, Minnesota in August 1994.

This item also exists in the form of an oral joke. Here is a version collected in Berkeley in 1994: A blonde is speeding down the highway when she is pulled over by a policeman. She asks him if there is any way she could get out of the ticket. The policeman starts to undo his belt and unzips his fly when she says, "Oh no, not the breathalizer test again!"

The variation in the four cartoon versions is extensive. The uniform of the policeman, the depiction of the woman, the police car or motorcycle, and many other details are strikingly different.

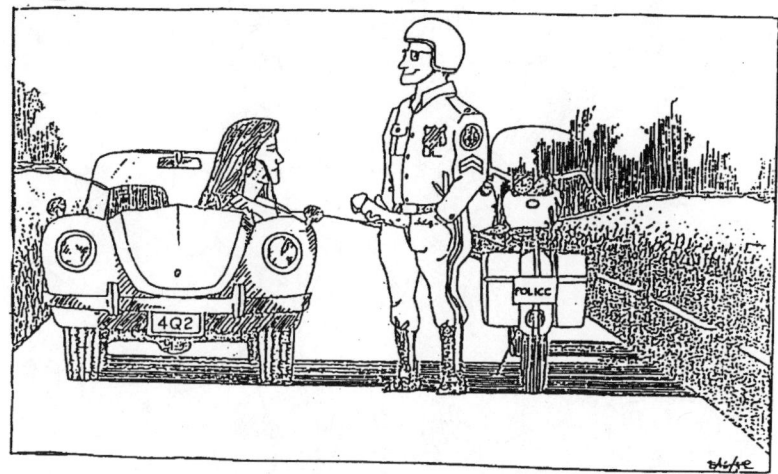

ARE YOU SURE THAT'S A BREATHALIZER??!!

162. Next Time, Use All of Your Fingers

Policemen can be overly aggressive to men as well as women. In the following cartoon collected in the San Francisco Bay Area in 1991, a man with unkempt hair, barefoot, and wearing a flower shirt evidently used only one finger in waving at the police officer. While police officers are trained not to overreact to taunts and gibes, they may, as humans, lose their tempers on occasion.

163. Are You Stuck?

Policemen are charged with regulating traffic and investigating traffic accidents. In the following cartoon, collected in Las Vegas in June 1994, a police officer asks a question of a truck driver when the answer is patently obvious, engendering a flippant smart aleck response from the potbellied, cigar-chomping, tattooed driver. For a verbal version, see Karen Warner, *500 Great Bartender's Jokes* (New York: Penguin, 1993), 171.

164. Can I Have a Grant?

In centuries past, artists, composers, and writers depended upon the largesse of individual patrons to support their creative activities. While this made it possible for talented individuals to accomplish their goals, it often required obsequious, fawning behavior, sometimes to the point of inhibiting the artistic expression. For example, artists were more or less obliged to include a portrayal of their sponsor, or a member of their patron's family, in the final painting.

In modern times, support for the arts often comes from either the government, wealthy or corporate donors, or foundations. It is an updated form of the patron system, though, the *noblesse oblige* is often stimulated by the added incentive of federal tax reductions. In the following ironic parody, an anti-establishment artist seeks financial aid from the very establishment he attacks. It was collected in Berkeley in July 1996, *from an artist.*

165. Deadline?

The attempt to impose time restrictions on artists is a commonplace complaint among creative individuals. One cannot, it is argued, insist that artistic inspiration be produced on command or completed within a fixed period of time. The following cartoon, collected in Berkeley in February 1990, comments on this issue. Set in a monastery where one assumes that the pace of life is relatively slow and the environment serene, a monk, working on an illuminated manuscript that requires painstaking meticulous attention to detail, is shocked by an unexpected request, so shocked that he indulges in an unholy expletive. For another version, see RIF, 154.

Deadline?
Nobody told me anything about a fucking deadline!

166. Help Wanted Male

A widespread fear among college students concerns the question of whether they will find suitable and rewarding employment upon graduation. Will they have the necessary qualifications for a challenging and well-paying position? There is a traditional folk paradigm that articulates this concern, especially for students who have majored in the humanities or social sciences:

> Science graduates ask: Why does it work?
>
> Engineering graduates ask: How does it work?
>
> Business majors ask: How much does it cost?
>
> Liberal arts graduates ask: Do you want fries with that?

The following folk cartoon sequence was collected in San Francisco from a P.G. and E. employee in September 1989. In another version (not presented here) the reference to P.G. and E. is replaced by the applicant responding to the "experience" question by saying: "I have a Master's degree and two years of Social Work." The cartoon makes a pretty explicit reference to one of the twelve labors of Hercules in classical Greek mythology. The fifth labor was one of the most demeaning ones; it involved cleaning out the stables of Augeas. In this modern update of the Augean stable episode, the animals are horses, not cattle. Still, the slang expression of "shit-work" or the euphemistic equivalent "scutwork" is typically used to refer to the menial tasks assigned to entry-level personnel, regardless of their educational achievements.

167. Application for Pardon

Americans, with their penchant for future orientation combined with a lesser appreciation for the past, generally tend to forgive and forget criminal behavior. "Let bygones by bygones" is a familiar motto. This had led, in some instances, to seemingly more concern for the welfare of the criminal than for the criminal's victims. Whether it is this apparent tendency toward lenience or a physical problem caused by severe overcrowding in prisons (or perhaps a combination of both), the public perceives that murderers, rapists, child molesters, and other felons are often released or pardoned after having served only a small fraction of the original sentence imposed.

The following item comments on the apparent ease with which even hardened repeat offenders can appeal for reduced sentences, if not outright release from prison. It was collected in Decatur, Alabama in February 1979.

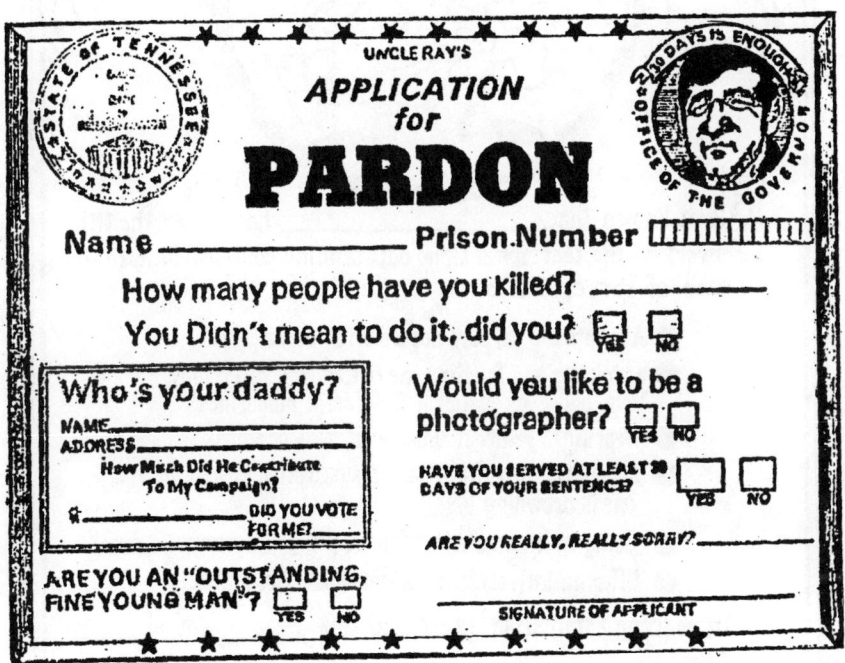

168. Pervert of the Year Award

In the context of greater media attention being devoted to criminals than to their victims, the following parody of award citations, collected in Mountain View, California, in the late 1980s, lists some of the most common forms of so-called indecent behavior.

PERVERT OF THE YEAR AWARD

Be it known that _____ has earned the title "Pervert of the Year for making outstanding contributions to the cause of Perversion by:

- Attempting to play doctor with strangers.
- Wrinkling and fondling the centerfolds of Playboy, Viva, and even National Geographic magazines.
- Wearing a raincoat whether it rains or shines.
- Attempting mouth-to-mouth resuscitation even when no one is drowning.
- Going on "moon shots" without being an astronaut.
- Offering little old ladies a seat while you're still in it.

In obscene admiration, presented this _____ day of _____ 19___ By _____
National Alliance of Perverts

169. The Perfect Man

From a stereotypical female perspective, a perfect man reduced to his simple essentials would consist of just a phallus and a money-producing anus. The cartoon, collected in Las Vegas, Nevada, in June 1994, is an analog to "The Perfect Woman," who consists of only breasts, vagina, buttocks, and legs (see WY, 57). For other photocopier allusions to the money-feces equation, see NT, 403.

170. Waiting . . . for the Perfect Man

Perfection in a mate, in ideal terms, may be well worth waiting for. But in practice, perfection may prove to be so rare or elusive as to be virtually nonexistent. The following cartoon, collected in Los Angeles in 1995, suggests the fate of any woman hoping to find perfection. The cobweb detail hints that, even after death, perfection has still not arrived. The bench setting also hints at a passive role for women, who are supposed to wait to be picked up by the perfect male rather than actively going out and looking for such an unlikely desideratum. For another photocopier item utilizing a skeleton to signal the elapse of a great deal of time, see WY, 203–4; for another instance of a cobweb symbolizing the same, see NT, 178.

171. Perfection

The definition of "perfection" can be delineated in words rather than pictures. The following folk poem, collected in Chicago in July 1991, provides a succinct portrait of an ideal woman—from a limited male perspective.

PERFECTION

I found the perfect woman,

I could not ask for more,

She's deaf and dumb and oversexed,

and owns a liquor store.

172. The Little Woman

Part of the male and female stereotypes in American folklore refers to relative physical size. It is the "*big* man" and the "*little* woman." The size differential is obviously related to traditional status hierarchy. In the following folk cartoon, the little woman turns out to have a big mouth, but its size is depicted as having been stretched to accommodate the large phallus of her husband. The cartoon also plays on the taboo theme of fellatio, which is not normally discussed in everyday discourse.

The first version was collected in Wilmington, Delaware in December 1990; the second from Savage, Minnesota in August 1994. The latter puts the caption in the mouth of a doctor, which presumably makes the scenario somewhat more plausible. For an earlier cartoon employing a similar caption but featuring a tiny woman with a normal-sized mouth, see J. M. Elgart, *Furthermore Over Sexteen* (New York: Elgart, 1956), 153.

"And this must be the little woman."

173. The Perfect Day

There is apparently no limit to male fantasy! Fellatio is just the beginning, as the following daily schedule of activities attests. Abundant sex, easy money, fine food and drink, not to mention a yacht, and a chauffeur-driven limousine are all requirements for a hedonistically ideal routine. The following item was collected from a Swiss bank in Geneva in 1989.

THE PERFECT DAY

6:00am	Arise
6:15-6:30	Blow Job
6:30-7:30	Run
7:30-8:00	Shower & Massage
8:00-8:15	Massive bowel movement (read sports section)
8:15	Limo arrives: Call broker on car phone. Recommends buying GM, instead short 100 S & P futures
8:30-12:00	Office Appearance
12:00-2:00	Lunch (thick rare steak, fries, cold Heineken)
2:00-3:00	Massage: Call broker, cover S & P futures for $15,000 profit
2:30-4:00	Nap on beach
4:00-5:00	Shower, shave, watch evening news, etc.
4:30-5:00	Limo arrives
5:15	Ice cold martinis on boat
5:30-8:00	Laker/Celtic game (Live on TV---NO women)
8:00-8:45	Dinner (barbecued albacore, salad, rare wines, followed by brandy and fine cigars)
8:45-9:55	Sex (with at least three women)
9:55-10:00	Women dress and leave
10:00	Bed (crisp white sheets, puffy new pillows)

174. Stop Exaggerating

Part of the male image of the perfect female refers to the desirability of a woman's having a small vagina. This is a common theme in jokes that invariably disparage a woman's large vagina (See #87 in this volume). Gershon Legman devoted a whole section of NLM (449–57) to "The Overlarge Vagina." The fear of this feature of female anatomy seems to be a projection of the male's fear that his own anatomical proportions are too small. Rather than accepting his own imperfection, he prefers to blame the female for *his* shortcoming.

The following folk cartoon illustrates this male fear. The first version was collected in Costa Mesa, California in 1976; it bears a name that appears to be Glenda Renfro, but it is highly unlikely that she is the original creator of the cartoon. Legman, for example, refers to earlier versions of the cartoon existing in 1951 (cf. NLM 452), in which either a railroad tie or an oar is employed. The second version was collected in Chicago in 1975. (Legman refers to this second version in RDJ, 678). For another photocopier tradition referring to a small vagina, see NT, 385.

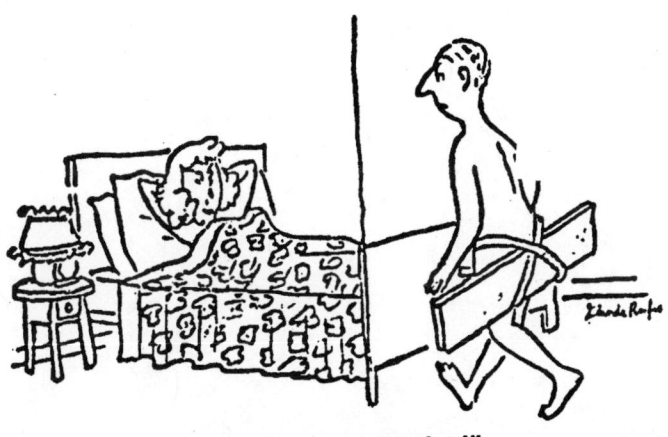

"Oh—stop exaggerating!"

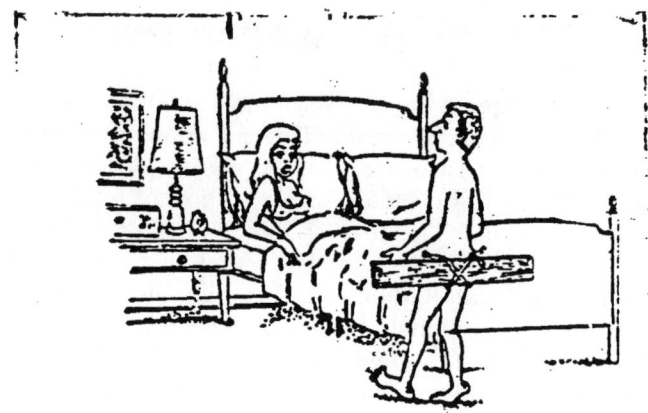

"Aw, come on Boyd, it's not THAT bad!"

175. Before It Gets Soft!

A male worries not only about the relative size of his organ, but also whether he can sustain an erection long enough to complete the sexual act. The fear of impotence is featured in the following traditional cartoon double entendre that goes back to the first half of the twentieth century. The first version was collected in Berkeley, California in the 1930s; the second was collected in the Police Athletic Club in San Francisco circa 1940. A third text, which utilizes snowmen rather than ice cream, was collected in Northridge, California in July 1996.

Quick! Before it MELTS!

176. No—I Can't Go Bowling Tonight

Whereas in the previous item it is the man who is ready for sexual activity and is dragging his female companion along for this purpose, in the following item, it is apparently the woman—who is ready for such activity—causing a man to cancel a bowling commitment (presumably with his male buddies). Although he uses verbiage normally referring to a woman's having her period, e.g., the word "moods," it may be to offer an acceptable excuse for staying home with the wife instead of going out with the boys. This item was collected from New Baltimore, Michigan in 1981.

177. Golf Balls

It could be argued that sports and heterosexual activity are in complementary distribution, meaning that they are mutually exclusive and that either can substitute for the other. Hence, wives of golfers are termed "golf widows." The term suggests that their husbands are as good as dead—as far as normal heterosexual relations are concerned—for the duration of their golf game. The connection between sexuality and golf is explicit in the following text collected in Iselin, New Jersey in July 1995. It definitely represents a male perspective inasmuch as the victimized wife appears willing to accept a limited number of adulterous infidelities. There may or may not be an intentional pun on the word "drawer." The wife is instructed not to look in her husband's drawer(s)!

It was the happy couple's wedding night, and the groom said to his wife, "Honey, you know I love you always, but I must ask you *never* to look in the bottom drawer of my dresser.

Ten years went by, and the wife never looked in that drawer. But one day, she could resist the temptation no longer. She opened the drawer to find three golf balls and $2,000 in cash. Of course, the woman could not resist confronting her husband.

The husband said, "Well, I'm sorry you looked in that drawer. But now that you have, I must admit the truth. You see, I put a golf ball into that drawer each time I was unfaithful to you." The wife thought about it, and although she was disappointed in her husband, it *had* been ten years, and she decided she could live with three infidelities.

"But what about the $2,000?" she then asked. "Oh," said the husband, "each time I had a dozen golf balls, I sold them."

178. Here, Take These

Many men become not just enthusiasts of a sport, but addicted fanatics. They may build their entire life around their preferred sporting activity. Golf provides a striking example of this behavior. One of the standard golf jokes has two men out on the golf course. Halfway through the game, a funeral cortege passes by on a nearby road. To one of the player's surprise, his partner stops playing, doffs his cap, and bows his head in momentary prayer. His astonished companion says, "I've been playing golf with you for a long time and I've never seen you do that before." His partner responds, "Well, I was married to her for twenty-five years." For other versions of this chestnut, see Ernest Forbes, *The Golfer's Gag Bag* (London: Futura, 1986, 10); and Stan McDougal, *The World's Greatest Golf Jokes* (Secaucus: Castle, 1980), 103.

The following item depicts the golfer making a choice consistent with the pattern delineated above. Both versions of this folk cartoon were collected in Chicago in 1994.

"Here, take these. I'm going back to get my wife."

326   Why Don't Sheep Shrink When It Rains?

179. Footprints

In times of crisis, one often needs help to survive. It is precisely at those moments when men may seek divine intervention or aid. Men are comforted by the sight of what they perceive as telltale signs of God's presence on earth. The following popular vignette with its uplifting, parable-like quality was collected in Santa Ana, California in January 1997. It is of interest that the "man" at the beginning becomes a "child" at the end. This would tend to support Freud's notion that God is to man as adult is to child. In other words, God is a glorified parent-surrogate, ready to pick up and comfort a child in distress. See Sigmund Freud, *The Future of an Illusion* (London: The Hogarth Press, 1949).

Footprints

One night a man had a dream. He dreamed he was walking along the beach with the LORD. Across the sky flashed scenes from his life. For each scene, he noticed two sets of footprints in the sand; one belonging to him, and the other to the LORD.

When the last scene of his life flashed before him, he looked back at the footprints in the sand. He noticed that many times along the path of his life there was only one set of footprints. He also noticed that it happened at the very lowest and saddest times in his life.

This really bothered him and he questioned the LORD about it. "LORD, you said that once I decided to follow you, you'd walk with me all the way. But I have noticed that during the most troublesome times in my life, there is only one set of footprints. I don't understand why when I needed you most you would leave me."

The LORD replied, "My precious, precious child, I love you and I would never leave you. During your times of trial and suffering, when you see only one set of footprints, it was then that I carried you."

— Author unknown —

180. The Beginning and the End

While religious faith may help man find his way through life, sometimes the problems of living are so horrific that one may wish that one had never been born. Of course, no one has that choice, that is, of never having been born, but the prevalence of suicide demonstrates the despair that some individuals feel. The following cartoon sequence articulates such a pessimistic worldview. It was collected in the early 1990s from a California hospital. For a version from 1977, see UFFC-PC, 91.

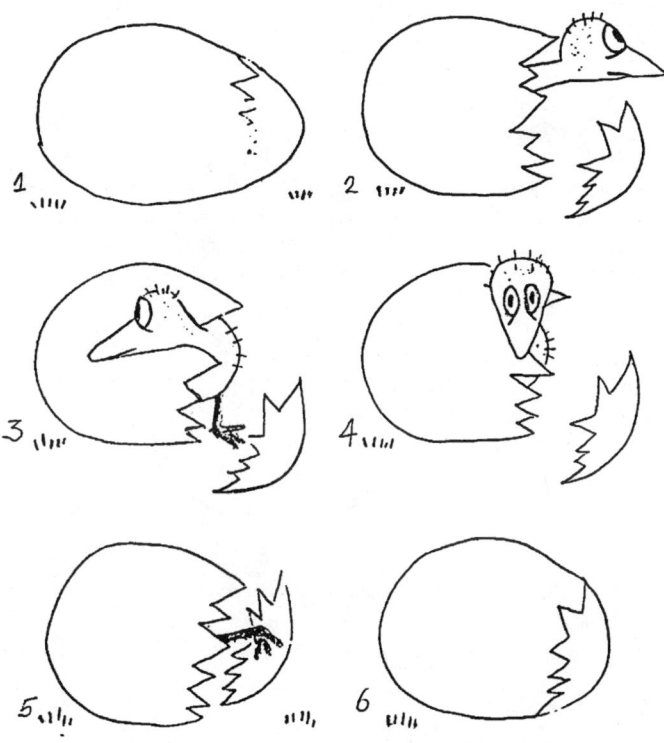

Conclusions

We confess our own astonishment and delight with the continued creation and verbal virtuosity of photocopier folklore. In our previous four collections, we presented more than six hundred examples of this vital tradition. One might have logically assumed that we had exhausted the corpus of this folklore genre. We believe this volume has demonstrated conclusively the falsity of any such assumption. The one hundred and eighty items we have documented here display the same incisive, witty articulation of key issues in American culture as the materials contained in our earlier volumes.

One reason for the proliferation of photocopier folklore is the important set of functions it serves. It encapsulates ethical issues; it skewers the frustrating forces encountered in the course of everyday life, and it provides welcome comic relief from the humdrum banalities arising from endless bureaucratic procedures. If laughter is cathartic, and we are fully persuaded that it is, the need for photocopier folklore is likely to accelerate in the twenty-first century. If urbanization and bureaucracy are on the increase, then new photocopier folklore is bound to arise.

Another possible explanation for the burgeoning quantity of photocopier folklore is the stunning impact of the Internet. For example, jokes formerly passed on orally on a one-to-one basis can now be sent instantaneously anywhere in the world to unnumbered individuals. What might have hitherto taken months to reach hundreds of individuals can now, in a matter of seconds, reach thousands or even millions of individuals. The combination of the Internet, e-mail, and the FAX machine have revolutionized the transmission of photocopier folklore. Many of the items in this volume, formerly transmitted by oral or typewritten means, are now sent by one of these new means of communication.

These modern machines have sometimes produced extended lists of items rather than single items. This, in effect, constitutes a form of folk collection that greatly facilitates the folklorist's task of sampling a particular item or joke cycle. On the other hand, one danger, from the folkloristic point of view, with the Internet, FAX, and e-mail "collections" is that the anonymous senders may include nontraditional items that must be distinguished from the truly traditional folklore, with its hallmark criteria of multiple existence and variation. Not everything transmitted by the computer, Internet, FAX, and e-mail is folklore! Even if it claims to be so.

The innovations in communications technology virtually guarantee a further proliferation of photocopier folklore, and this leads us to compare this type of folklore with the older, more traditional genres. For the past two centuries, folklorists have tended to concentrate on certain forms of folklore. One could even say that the study of orally transmitted epics, myths, ballads, and folktales has constituted the central focus of professional folklorists. But the truth is that there is a relatively finite number of epics in the world, myths in the world, ballads and folktales in the world. Some would argue that the corpus of 305 English and Scottish ballads, (the so-called Child ballad), is a closed one with no new traditional ballads being added to the canon. The same holds for magic folktales, that is, Aarne-Thompson tale types 300 to 749. In contrast, photocopier folklore is increasing in numbers by leaps and bounds. It is a live, energetic, vibrant folk form, and in that sense differs from some of the older, seemingly moribund traditions. This is not to denigrate the power and beauty of traditional ballads and fairy tales. They will doubtless continue to delight and instruct generations to come. One cannot imagine little girls not encountering Cinderella (AT 510A)—although many of the traditional folktales are now filtered through mass media: Disney film versions or comic book or cartoon treatments.

There are, to be sure, traditional folklore forms that are every bit as popular as ever. One can find plenty of new folk speech, contemporary legends, proverbs, and jokes, among others. But it is our contention that no form of folklore surpasses photocopier folklore in its potential for growth in the future. What this means is that what was once considered to be a trivial and marginal area of folklore research is quite likely to become a major focus for folklorists of the twenty-first century.